CLEM SUNTER

The Casino Model

TAFELBERG
HUMAN & ROUSSEAU

First published in 1994 jointly by
Tafelberg Publishers Ltd, 28 Wale Street, Cape Town
and Human & Rousseau (Pty) Ltd,
State House, 3-9 Rose Street, Cape Town

Typeset in 10 on 13 pt Monotype Nimrod
Printed and bound by National Book Printers,
Goodwood, Cape, South Africa
First edition, first impression 1994

ISBN 0 624 03330 9

*To Margaret
and in memory of
Rick Lomba*

Contents

The casino model, 2

Now gold is the gambler, 2

The house take needs to be reasonable, 4

The casino overheads have to be cost effective
  and transparent, 5

The croupiers must be honest, 7

Casinos compete on competence and infrastructure, 8

Good casinos look at best practice elsewhere, 10

Casino operators don't gamble on their own tables, 12

The global economy is a three-tiered casino, 13

The odds should be fixed, 16

No uncertainty should surround ownership of chips, 16

Chips must be freely convertible into cash, 17

Casinos can't afford too many holidays, 19

Gamblers seek security, 20

The casino must be open to all, 21

The slots are not enough, 23

Karl was no gambler, 25

Good casinos encourage successful gamblers, 27

There has to be a dream machine, 28

Rich casinos cannot afford to be surrounded by poor
  casinos, 29

Casino operators shouldn't get too close to the gamblers, 30

The casino is open 24 hours a day, 32

Economics and gambling don't yet mix, 34

Gamblers help each other, 37

A casino is a closed system, 38

A high house take encourages informal games, 39

Gambling is a great leveller, 40

Gambling is no sin, 41

Aces can be trumped, 47

Kids should be taught to gamble, 51
Gamblers keep opposites in mind, 53
Good gamblers see patterns others don't, 57
Good gamblers know their limits, 59
Gamblers spread their bets, 64
If there's no other way, gamblers go for the long shot, 67
A bet is a bet is a bet, 68
Gamblers like to narrow the odds, 70
Cash is king, 75
For every bet there's an opportunity cost, 76
Every gambler has a misery curve, 78
The nuclear game is the deadliest of all, 88
Probabilities can be problematic, 90
Clumsy bluffs get called, 93
Gamblers are best at betting their own money, 95
Betting on credit is risky, 99
Charts are an art, 101
Advice to gamblers comes in threes, 104

This book has been written in praise of people who take risks. It therefore embraces almost everyone since, life being what it is, there is no easy and chanceless way to achieve goals – monetary or non-monetary. The future will always be "iffy".

The book is basically divided into two halves. The first half invokes a model to describe the realities of an economy and the proper role of government in looking after the economy. It is appropriately called the "casino model", because much of what goes on in the economy is merely a refined form of gambling. The parallels will become obvious as details of the model emerge.

The second half of the book explores the mind of a risk-taker – be he or she an entrepreneur, a gambler or just a bold person ready to take up the challenge of change and react positively to it. There are diversions into explanations of the more important yardsticks used by business to assess projects and into revealing the kind of probabilities associated with various games of chance. At the very end, readers are provided with some golden rules to improve their technique of choosing between options and generally handling the uncertainty of the future.

I would like to single out for thanks Pat Meneghini for typing the manuscript and Koos Human, Lappies Labuschagne, Hans Büttner, Jürgen Fomm and Jill Martin for their invaluable assistance in the preparation of the book.

O.K. Let's deal.

The casino model

In this model, a national economy is viewed as a local casino. The entrepreneurs, big and small, are the clientele of the casino – the gamblers. The government is the casino operator, the civil servants the casino staff. The shareholders who own the casino are the population at large. They have the opportunity of dismissing or retaining the casino operator at least once every five years when a general election takes place.

Government revenue or taxation is the house take of the casino. Profits of the private sector are the winnings of the gamblers. From this simple model, a multiplicity of interesting implications follow . . .

Now gold is the gambler

Casino managements come and go; they all have their own special ideas about running the place, but the gamblers are the ones who through word of mouth give the casino a "hot" reputation or not. No one has yet written the master work on why fashions begin, how they spread and why they die out. Nevertheless, it does seem that such a cycle involves a moment in time when the number of devotees passes through a critical level and the fashion turns temporarily into a "craze". The growth in popularity from then on is exponential and autonomous (in that it feeds on itself).

Economies go through the same celebrity cycles. The 1980s saw the peak of the Japanese cycle where every conceivable management textbook extolled the virtues of the Japanese way. Now the spotlight has moved on to Indonesia, Malaysia, India and China. In the last century Britain could do no wrong. Before that it was Spain, Portugal and Holland. After Britain,

America. Nations go through extraordinary phases of wealth creation when the common people are swept up in a collective wave of inventiveness, resourcefulness and mutual inspiration. The political leaders at the time may have something to do with releasing these sudden bursts of energy, but more often than not they arise from within the populace for reasons unknown. How else can one explain the Australian domination of tennis, the British domination of "pop music", the American domination of space in the 1960s or the Kenyan domination of long-distance running in the 1980s and 1990s?

The election of a new government in any country is treated as a most newsworthy event. It is as if this in itself will alter the course of history. Yet, when a casino changes hands, it hardly merits attention. Banner headlines are reserved for the gamblers – like the one who "broke the bank at Monte Carlo". So why is it that politicians get the limelight and very little is done to illuminate the entrepreneurs who really can change a nation's destiny? Strange indeed. South Africa had its own flash of entrepreneurial energy in the 1880s and 1890s when Johannesburg was a dusty town full of prospectors and miners and people setting up businesses to satisfy their needs (including Charles Glass). Somehow the institutionalisation of life over the following hundred years, though it has led to a most successful and modern economy, has never quite re-created that initial surge of activity. Perhaps now is the time for renewal, given that the casino is under new and legitimate management. Fresh faces will be seen at the tables, new games will be introduced, and the established players will be challenged for their seats in the best corner of the room. We need another "gold rush" to celebrate the new South Africa – but this time the gold will be the ideas of the younger generation.

The house take needs to be reasonable

Without gamblers a casino doesn't exist. All the salaries of the casino's staff, the upkeep of the casino itself, the surplus that the casino makes for its shareholders, come out of the house take. If the house take is considered too high by the gamblers – if they get the feeling that they're being ripped off – then the casino simply loses its clients and eventually closes down. In the interim period before closure, the casino runs into the vicious circle of declining turnover forcing the casino to raise the percentage of the take on each game to cover its overheads. This frightens more clients away, forcing the casino to offer even less respectable odds to the players and so on in a downward spiral.

The reverse is also true. If the casino becomes increasingly popular, the casino operator can afford to lower the percentage take and make the games more attractive, which bring in even more clients. Economists call this the "elasticity of demand".

The single zero-double zero controversy overseas illustrates this point. Some foreign casinos have only one zero on a roulette wheel while others have two. The double zero gives less favourable odds to the gamblers. They therefore favour casinos where only one zero is used on the roulette wheel. The same condition applies to slot machines which can be programmed for higher or lower payouts. If a casino gets the reputation of mean programming of slot machines, the customers will try their luck elsewhere.

Governments must exhibit the same degree of caution regarding tax rates. If they do, and maintain modest levels, they may be pleasantly surprised that their overall revenue rises faster than if they had applied a more severe tax code. This is because economic growth, which is a measure of the increase in number and size of bets being successfully placed in an economy during a quarter or year, is faster in a low as opposed to a high tax environment. The sheer volume of transactions rises so quickly that the modesty of the tax deduction is over-

4

whelmed by the increase in activity which is liable to tax. It is no coincidence that in the fastest growing economies in the world – mainly in the Far East – tax as a percentage of GNP is lowest (around 20 per cent is the norm).

However, as somebody ruefully said to me the other day: "South Africa is unique. Given how highly we're taxed at the moment, it's already a casino with a triple zero. Hence, it's better to buy into the casino and be part of the government than to be an entrepreneur and gamble in it." He was joking, but many a truth is said in jest!

The casino overheads have to be cost effective and transparent

On the basis of the previous principle that the house take needs to be reasonable, the expenses of the casino must be prioritised, rigorously kept in check, audited and published. The number of staff, their remuneration, the costs of maintaining the building, rooms, tables and slot machines – all these have to be carefully controlled. If the casino is saddled with interest-bearing loans, then the interest on those loans is part of the overhead too.

Moreover, should the senior management of the casino appear to be leading too flamboyant a life style with limousines, estates, jets and other flashy possessions, not only the gamblers (entrepreneurs) but also the shareholders (public) will be suspicious that their money is being illegitimately siphoned off by the operators to line their own pockets. So the books of the casino ought to be open to all in order to combat any suspicion that the house take is abnormally high (the concern of the gamblers) or is being wasted on inefficient outlays, bloated staff counts and *la dolce vita* of the top people running the business (the concern of the shareholders).

Politicians need to develop a cost-benefit approach to the

state budget. This form of analysis should be used to pinpoint those areas where tax revenue can most usefully be applied. Moreover, there is an important difference between tax that is used to reimburse the head-office-type overhead expenses of government – central administration, the upkeep and rent of buildings, the interest on government debt and so on – and the tax used to provide direct benefits to the public in the fields of education, health, social welfare, clean potable water, public works programmes, etc. The former is the equivalent of the expenses of the casino, the latter the dividends to the public as shareholders.

The overriding message, though, is that all the marvellous things that politicians promise can only be carried out within the constraints of what keeps the customers coming to the casino and placing their bets. Nor can the politicians borrow their way out of trouble, because the interest payable on what they borrow immediately puts the squeeze on their plans for expenditure elsewhere. Like it or not, the entrepreneurs who gamble are at the head of the food chain. Without them, all the intentions to undertake the good works that are a necessary condition for a decent society and a high quality of life for all will come to nought, because no money is available to fund the programmes. Profit has to be made by businesses, income has to be earned and spent by individuals for tax to be raised. Finally, accurate and easy-to-understand state accounts must be furnished regularly to the public for them to study. For the public are the ultimate shareholders of the country.

Possibly the best way to get parliamentarians to focus on what they are there for – achieving a high level of economic growth with minimum state overheads – is to pay them a bonus linked to published GNP growth figures. This is not unreasonable, as you can be sure that the remuneration of a casino operator is linked to the casino's performance.

The croupiers must be honest

Allied to the previous point about keeping casino expenses down, the croupiers have to be "straight". Otherwise nasty things happen. The croupiers will collude with the gamblers in order for the latter to reap illegitimate rewards from the casino, the spoils being shared between them. The upshot is that the casino loses revenue and the honest gamblers suffer as the casino has to make up these unauthorised losses by raising the house take as a whole. Another consequence of employing croupiers who do not meet high standards of honesty is that one has in addition to hire an excessive number of people to watch the croupiers and a multitude of others to watch the watchers and so on up the line. This adds mightily to the overheads.

Generally, if the market finds out that the casino has corrupt croupiers this will deter the upright members of the public from coming to the casino. In the United States, the association of some casinos with the Mafia has tarnished the industry for years, and it must have had a dampening effect on the customer base. Las Vegas is after all not Disneyland.

The fact is that official corruption is probably the greatest threat facing most national economies, developed and developing alike. Unfortunately, there are plenty of unscrupulous entrepreneurs out there seeking to get an edge on their competition by offering bribes in exchange for favours from those writing the rules of the game. No society is corruption-free, but a country that gets a name for percentage commissions, kickbacks, untraceable bank accounts and the like is given a wide berth by the mainstream of world-class companies who are the biggest punters around. Moreover, corruption impedes domestic business in that it is a secret additional tax which raises the required rate of return on any new investment planned by an entrepreneur. The task of auditor-general is therefore one of the most important in government today. Crucial too are a fearless political opposition, a vigilant press and an independent judiciary.

Casinos compete on competence and infrastructure

Good gamblers don't go to casinos with tacky decor, inept croupiers, bolshy catering staff, wildcat strikes, impromptu demonstrations, lousy food and bad accommodation. Can you imagine how impressed gamblers would be if the power supply was intermittent and the lights occasionally went out when the wheel was in spin or their cards were on the table? Regular and successful punters like to gamble in nice surroundings with dependable service. They like to have pleasant distractions when they're away from the tables. That's why the best casinos are frequently located in attractive places – by the sea, close to a game park, near entertainment centres – and the hotels that go with these casinos offer superlative service. It is no coincidence that of the ten largest hotels in the world, nine are in Las Vegas.

The staff in the top casinos are highly trained, polite facilitators to the customers. The croupiers know everything that opens and shuts about the rules of the game which they're overseeing, so that no extraordinary situation can upset them. They're scrupulously honest (see the section on honesty of croupiers), they're quick to answer a client's questions and meet his or her requests with a minimum of bureaucracy and officialdom. They give the unswerving impression that they are there to serve the gamblers and enjoy doing it. However, they have also been taught to react swiftly when a customer gets out of hand and starts bending the rules or infringing upon the freedom of other customers. They are experts at containing a potentially ugly situation with the least amount of fuss.

As mentioned at the outset, the equivalent to the casino staff in the real economy is the civil service, whilst the hotels and ancillaries represent the general infrastructure. The first impressions of a country for many foreign business people are very important. They are impressed by civil servants of high calibre who speak the same commercial language and don't shower them with red tape. Hence, given the point that government revenue (the house take) has to be reasonable, it is far better to have a small civil service of top-rate people than a large civil service of mediocre individuals who are simply beneficiaries of a government decision to fulfil the role of employer of last resort. As far as infrastructure is concerned, business people want clean and efficient airports, reliable aircraft, service-oriented hotels, well-maintained roads, faxes and telephones that work, 24-hour news of the markets and so on.

Singapore is a splendid example of a country that is very conscious of the initial impression it makes on visitors. Flowers, the absence of litter and customer dedication are just some of the features that strike anyone arriving at the airport for the first time. But one experience I had there on a recent visit says it all. On my first afternoon, I left the hotel and went for a jog down the main street at 4 p.m. I tripped over a slightly raised paving stone next to a bus stop and sat down on some nearby steps to catch my breath. A Chinese concierge of the office building to which the steps belonged rushed down the steps and asked if I was all right. I said yes and continued on my way. The following morning at 8 a.m. I decided to repeat the same route and this time I was prepared. There was the bus stop, there the office building, so there must be the raised paving stone. But, lo, when I arrived at the spot, can you imagine my amazement when I found that the entire area had been repaved! I even stooped down to examine the new cement and sand surrounding each paving stone. The concierge had obviously informed the appropriate municipal department about my accident shortly after it had happened and they had taken action that same night. This example neatly illustrates the type of accountability required to keep entrepreneurs coming again and again to place bets in another country's economy.

The Singaporean example is in direct contrast to an experience I had at Waterloo station in London in December 1992. Because of icy conditions, many of the trains departing from Waterloo for southern destinations had been cancelled. I looked up at the departure board for the time and the platform relating to the next train to Portsmouth Harbour. No information was available. I approached a station official for assistance and he referred me to the departure board. When I said that the reason for my asking him was that the departure board offered no clues, he replied brusquely: "Who knows with all these cancellations, but try Platform 9. The train will probably leave at 5:50 p.m.". I walked to Platform 9 and a donnish-looking man was standing there in one of those tweed jackets with leather elbows. I asked him: "Is the train for Portsmouth Harbour leaving from this platform at 5:50?" His response showed his scholarly background: "If you rephrase that question to 'Do I believe that the train for Portsmouth Harbour leaves from this platform at 5:50 p.m.?' from past experience the answer is yes!" Other would-be passengers joined us on the platform, but at 5:50 a garbled announcement came over the loudspeakers that the train to Portsmouth Harbour would only arrive at 6:00 and would leave from Platform 6. Everybody but my scholarly man dashed off to Platform 6. True to his belief, he stayed. So, therefore, did I. And sure enough the train arrived at Platform 9!

Good casinos look at best practice elsewhere

Gamblers are footloose and fancy-free. They will shop around for the place they can get the best odds, the place where they feel most welcome, the place where there is a minimum of red tape to lay a bet and the place where there are easy credit terms. Casinos compete for gamblers and they have to adopt the best practices around to attract them. Good casino operators are therefore anything but smug, complacent and arrogant. They tour the other successful casinos to ascertain what their strengths are and then adapt these strengths to their own situation. Apart from mimicking others, a leading-edge casino will of course also look for completely original ways of grabbing extra market share from its competitors. Thereby such an exceptional casino becomes a blueprint for others to follow.

In the casino model, each country is a casino competing for the world-class players. They offer tax holidays, tax rebates, investment allowances, investment grants, low inflation, modest wage levels, high productivity, political and labour stability, etc. American states vie with each other over the carrots they dangle to attract a Japanese or European company to their turf. Perhaps South African provinces will do the same (like their cities did with the chance to host the 2004 Olympic Games). Nevertheless, tensions arise with local residents if countries go too far overboard in trying to woo overseas gamblers. The local residents begin to feel that they are being elbowed out of their own market, one in which they should have a greater right to gamble than strangers from abroad. Like all else, a balance is required between the need to obtain top skills and state-of-the-art technology from overseas and promotion of domestic business, particularly small business.

Now that most economic-growth-impeding ideologies in the world have been discarded, the formula for economic success is spreading at the speed of light to all corners of the earth. The world economy is probably in its most competitive state than at any other time in this century. Open trade and modern technology have made an increasing number of jobs internationally contestable. A local authority in the north of England recently awarded the contract of keeping its records up to date to a Taiwanese firm. Every evening, the day's transactions are downloaded from computers in Newcastle-on-Tyne to computers in Taipei where overnight they are sorted out into the appropriate files and returned the following morning. Previously, only a local firm could have performed a service like that.

In addition, there are attractive options everywhere for global investors. Against that, South Africa offers the best infrastructure on the African continent. If we follow the best practices of the "Asian dragons", the response from the international business community should be very positive. After all, we are the stepping stone to the markets in the rest of sub-Saharan Africa.

11

Casino operators don't gamble on their own tables

It would raise the eyebrows of most gamblers if a casino operator became a serious and regular punter at his own tables. It would certainly be perceived as a conflict of interest, and there would always be the suspicion that the croupiers were rigging the odds for him because he was their boss.

Likewise, nationalisation puts a government in the same invidious and somewhat ambivalent position. On a different tack, tax payers don't pay tax to have the government gamble with their money on business ventures. They pay tax for it to be put into education, health, infrastructure, welfare, etc. If the government borrows the money to satisfy its gambling instinct, it is even worse. Interest on loans is certain, whereas the financial return on commercial projects is not.

Anyway, government ministers and civil servants were not elected or appointed to their positions because of their prowess on the gaming tables of business. Around the world, therefore, the track record of businesses owned by the state and of projects initiated by the state has been dismal. It normally ends up with money having to be switched from the legitimate areas of the state's budget into subsidising losses caused by rash commercial decisions made by politicians "in the national interest". It is hardly surprising, therefore, that privatisation of state assets is being pursued by such a wide variety of governments.

The global economy
is a three-tiered casino

There are three levels of gambling in the world economy today. On the ground level is the global exchange of goods and services. When money is bet on this floor of the casino, it takes the form of physical investment in plant, machinery, land and buildings, mines, etc.

On the first floor are the stock, bond, commodity and foreign exchange markets. The fund managers, famous for the scarlet braces that hitch up their trousers, switch from one game to another. They hunt for the next market to give them high returns which will retain or improve their funds' ranking in the performance league. They show no sentiment for any particular market, joining it for the "play" and leaving it when the "play" is over. Far greater sums of money cross the tables of the casino each month in these rooms than on the ground floor, measured in trillions rather than billions of dollars. When the punters on this floor get really active, they can cause sudden stock market crashes like the one in October 1987, as well as sudden depreciations of currency, which reveal how powerless governments can be in the face of market runs on their currency. How many finance ministers in the world rue the day that they put their hands on their hearts and said that their country was not devaluing its currency! Really, said the market and promptly humbled them.

The first floor has also given birth to an interesting paradox called "the paradox of volatile stability". Many observers criticise the freedom that speculators have in switching vast sums of one currency into another by simply pressing a computer key, because it causes considerable volatility in currency markets. In fact, the fear of instant retribution from the market in the wake of a stupid policy decision acts as a very effective brake on politicians. It limits their tendency to ignore the realities of the international economic game in their pursuit of domestic popularity. A sharp rap on the knuckles imposes a discipline and stability which didn't exist twenty years ago when governments had been getting away with bad policies for years.

The second floor of the casino has just been added. It is the "derivatives" market. Instead of buying or selling actual shares, bonds, commodities or currencies, you enter into "forward contracts" under which you're obligated to buy or sell at some future date. Or you buy or sell the "option" to do something at a future date. Or you enter a "swap" where you exchange your fixed interest loan for somebody else's variable interest loan or vice versa. Or, more exotically, you agree to an option at a future date to swap your positions (called "swaptions"). The derivatives market is full of slang terms like "in the money", "out of the money", "roll-over", "minimax", "knockout", "delta" and the like. Vastly complex mathematical models are used to compute the risk of taking any position in the derivatives market and for monitoring the risk of holding on to that position and for assessing whether you should take other positions to offset the risk of your original position. The masters of these mathematical models are called "rocket scientists" in recognition of the fact that, because it's such a new market, there are very few people around who have a complete grasp of the odds associated with any bets made there.

The danger of gambling on this second floor of the casino is illustrated by the magnitude of losses of some of the players. In 1993, a Chilean trader employed by the state-owned copper producer lost $207 million by speculating on copper futures. In Germany, a giant conglomerate bet the wrong way on oil futures and lost $1,3 billion. Without proper financial checks and controls in place, one trader in one transaction now has the ability to neutralise the annual profit made by 100 000 workers – or to double it. Several respected investment bankers have therefore expressed their alarm about the addition of the derivatives floor to the casino on the grounds that all three floors have interlocking consequences for one another. Losses in futures or options can cause sales of shares and bonds on the first floor, thus depressing the markets there; or they can cause bankruptcies of firms producing goods and services on the ground floor, leading to economic recession and loss of jobs. Nevertheless, the linkages can be positive as well. Smart "hedging" on the second floor can act as an insurance policy for an industry on the ground floor should that industry go through hard times (as the gold mining industry did in South Africa from 1990 to mid-1993).

The growing power and flexibility of computers has enormously accelerated the pace with which bets can be laid, and increased the magnitude of the bets themselves. Some American merchant banks are spending up to $1 billion a year installing extra computer capacity to cope with the complexity of gambling in the financial "cyberspace" of the first and second floors. Computerised trading has become such a powerful force in the market that the New York Stock Exchange has instituted "shock absorbers" and "circuit breakers" to limit the rate of descent of the index in the event that the drop exceeds a certain number of points in a single session. This is to stop a runaway fall when an avalanche of "sell" orders hits the market from computers programmed to sell at the same price point.

In summary, the evolution of global markets has made life for the ordinary business person orders of magnitude more complicated than it was for previous generations of entrepreneurs. The choices of how you structure a bet before you place it on the table are mind-boggling. Revenue is no longer simply the money you get when you sell the product. You can sell the product forward; or you can buy an option to "put" the product to another party at a certain date at a certain price. Obviously, you will exercise the option if at the date the option expires the current market price of your product is below the "put" price. Costs are not what they were either. For instance, you can stabilise the cost of your raw materials by forward purchases or by buying the option to "call" for the raw materials from another party at a certain price at a certain date. Thus, there is no place for amateurish gamblers in this three-tiered casino. Professionalism and experience are the qualities which make a gambler a consistent winner. But hasn't this always been true in a game of poker?

The odds should be fixed

When a croupier says *"faites vos jeux"* at roulette and you accordingly place your bets on the table, you would be stunned if he changed the odds arbitrarily against you once the wheel was spinning. If he offered the excuse that the casino was going broke or the croupiers were poorly paid and management had decided to increase the house take to rectify the situation, you would not be impressed. Indeed you would wish to declare the bet null and void.

So it is with embarking on a project and the rate of tax applicable to a project. Business does not want to put billions of rands on the table after carefully calculating the prospective after-tax rewards only to find once the project has been commissioned that the tax rate has changed for the worse. In a sense there has to be an unwritten covenant between government and business that the rules of the game remain the same. Whatever the relevant tax code is, it is stable.

Nothing will kill off investment more quickly than uncertainty about future tax rates. How can anyone gamble if they can't be sure about what they get back if they win? Obviously, a government is entitled to set the rules under which entrepreneurs operate. But chopping and changing the rules afterwards is the quickest way to close the casino down.

No uncertainty should surround ownership of chips

Allied to the previous point about odds, imagine a punter who has played roulette for several hours and won handsomely. He has a large pile of chips in front of him. Can you now imagine how surprised he would be if the croupier scooped up some of his winnings and said they belonged to the house? He would regard this as straight theft.

Even if the croupier muttered something about the casino introducing a wealth tax or that the circumstances in which the chips had been purchased in the first place by the punter were questionable and therefore some had to be returned to the casino, these would hardly be considered satisfactory answers. In reality, this action would send such a message to all the other customers that they would do everything they could to cash in their chips and go to another casino. Potential new customers would be put off completely.

Private property rights are fundamental to the running of a successful economy. Financial ruin awaits the state that tampers with them. Even the threat of taking away property introduces a cloud of uncertainty into the risk-reward equation, causing new investment to plummet. What entrepreneur is going to put up a new plant or seek to improve an existing one if he is worried that the state might confiscate it? What foreign investor is going to use his own currency to purchase chips to play in a casino which may then dispute his right to those chips or the winnings he makes out of them? None!

Chips must be freely convertible into cash

Suppose a gambler has a winning run in the casino, but when he goes to cash in his chips at the till, he's told that either none or only some of them are convertible into cash. The cashier suggests that he either spends them on a meal and drinks in the casino or returns to the tables and gambles some more. Neither suggestion would be attractive. He would want his money now.

But this is the prospect facing any foreign investor when restrictions are placed on remitting dividends from his investment in another country back to his home base. Equally this is the prospect facing a local company that wishes to reinvest overseas some of the profits it has made in the domestic market, but is blocked from doing so by exchange control.

A far harsher restriction would be to lock the doors of the casino to restrict the flow of gamblers into and out of the casino. Governments have been known to do just that with immigration and emigration controls. Or they may subject any decision by foreigners wishing to invest locally or by locals wishing to invest overseas to a myriad of bureaucratic regulations and licences. Experience has shown that doormen are very susceptible to bribes when they wield too much power over who can enter or leave the casino.

Obviously, for a casino to be popular, punters must feel that there is absolute certainty about exchanging cash for chips and back again and that they are free to enter and leave the casino as they wish. A related issue is that punters do not want the value of their chips to decline in whatever currency they ultimately intend to take their winnings. Devaluation of a nation's currency is therefore a two-edged sword. On the one hand, it does give local exporters a temporary advantage in foreign markets because they can sell their goods more cheaply there. Domestic producers also benefit from the fact that competing imports become more costly. Let it be said, though, that the extra boost given to domestic inflation by devaluation closes this window of opportunity fairly quickly. On the other hand, overseas companies are going to be a lot more chary about putting money into a country where their winnings are expected to devalue at a rate which offers little return on their original hard currency investment. This is also the reason why they steer clear of countries who've got themselves too heavily in debt. Any heavy repayment of capital scheduled in the future casts a shadow over the foreign exchange reserves of those countries.

Worldwide, if one wishes to compare economies on some form of international rating scale, the strength of a country's currency is one of the best indicators. The consequence of companies flocking from overseas to invest in a particular economy will – in terms of normal supply/demand considerations – be to increase the price of the chips in that economy in foreign currency terms. If they're leaving in droves, the opposite will happen.

A final point on exchange control. It encourages young local entrepreneurs to relocate physically overseas as that is the only way to build up a foreign bank balance. Countries cannot afford to lose this young talent – it's a great deal more costly than losing capital. By allowing residents to hold their money in whatsoever currency they wish, where they wish, there's a greater chance that they will stay.

Casinos can't afford too many holidays

The more frequently a casino has to close because of public holidays, the lower the turnover and hence the house take for the year. Meanwhile, the overheads, which include the salaries of staff, renewal of buildings, etc., are unaffected by holidays and loom large in the overall cost structure. Only variable costs such as the cost of meals and drinks are saved. The net position is that a shutdown for even a day is very expensive.

The same applies to an economy. The cost of a day's shutdown of the South African economy is variously estimated to be somewhere between R1 billion and R1,5 billion. The tax on the level of output which is lost must be considerable. In turn, the lost tax makes it that much more difficult for a government to balance its books. Moreover, where holidays are granted more than once in a week or a fortnight, the stop/start pattern that prevails during the period affects more than the days concerned. When a business is running at full steam and its momentum is interrupted, it takes time to build up pressure in the boiler again and return to full speed.

All in all, statutory holidays for a country that wants to become a "winning nation" should be kept to a minimum.

Gamblers seek security

All gamblers want security. They don't want to walk out of the casino with their winnings and get mugged in the car park. Nor do they want bandits to come into the casino and hold them up as they're playing.

Law and order figures high on the list of most ordinary citizens. Yet it is that very aspect of society which is breaking down everywhere. Crime is ballooning because it is a deviant form of gambling. The risk of retribution has declined while the promise of rewards has increased. In Britain, 30 million crimes were committed last year, of which only two per cent led to conviction – 98 per cent went unpunished. Good odds for any criminal! Other places are getting fed up. In California, for example, a law has just been passed to redress the imbalance. Entitled "three strikes and you're out", it basically compels judges to give 25-year prison sentences (with no right of appeal) to criminals convicted of a third serious offence. Crime prevention measures – car immobilisers, house alarms, police foot patrols, gun control, community policing and neighbourhood watches – are also receiving major emphasis.

As soon as a neighbourhood becomes too rough, the entrepreneurs close their businesses and move out, while the shopkeepers put up the shutters and look for alternative premises. Every time one reads of another café owner being gunned down for the petty cash in his till, it leaves a very sick feeling inside. Civil society is held together by the interchange of goods and services between people of all trades and professions. As crime takes over and these threads snap, the community descends into poverty, hopelessness and violence. The crime bosses become the clientele of the casino and drive out the honest gamblers.

Casino operators beware! If you want your gamblers to be creative and happy and remain regular customers, they must play in an environment free of fear.

The casino must be open to all

Notwithstanding the advice just given, there is more to security than law and order. No casino in a relatively poor neighbourhood can afford to be an exclusive club for the rich minority. If the masses are turned away at the door for no apparent reason, the danger will always exist that they will come back and burn the casino down. In the United States in the 1980s, economic growth delivered 70 per cent of its benefits to the richest one per cent. A casino with that kind of limitation on wealth dispersion is awfully vulnerable. It will be plagued by social instability.

The casino therefore has to be open to all, and the conditions of entry easy to meet. Of course, there is the need for novices to acquire the skills to gamble. Fulfilling this need through training is the joint responsibility of the casino operator and the other experienced gamblers already playing in the casino. Both parties should bear in mind that it is infinitely preferable for the people who are not yet members of the club to join the other players in the casino who are producing wealth in the marketplace than become part of the casino overheads (by joining the civil service). In the long run, educating people to gamble is the only sustainable way to create millions of new jobs. The other option of increasing casino overheads eventually closes the casino down.

Besides training, any novice has to use considerable ingenuity in acquiring the initial chip to make the first wager. For most first-time businessmen and women the money is usually stumped up from their own or their family's savings or from private savings societies (*stokvels*). But to make the casino a universal one in South Africa will necessitate a great deal of creative thinking from banks and venture capital institutions to overcome the financial bottleneck. The entrepreneurs are there. They just don't have the money.

Even while the lowest rungs of the capital-funding ladder are being put in place to kick-start small business development, the higher rungs will need attention too. The original purpose behind the formation of limited liability companies was to spread the risk of any major project among the public at large, because the entrepreneur behind the project could not afford to take the risk fully on himself or herself – or did not possess the financial resources to do so. Each individual shareholder puts up a fraction of the project's overall cost in the form of a capital sum commensurate to his personal financial circumstances. Because he can only lose his contribution, and as such his liability is limited, he will be prepared to contribute. He certainly wouldn't be so willing to do so if the liability was open-ended – however small the risk. Certain members of Lloyds in London have received a very painful lesson in the concept of unlimited liability. This simple model of an entrepreneur floating a new company and inviting the public to subscribe for new shares in the company is the main driving force behind the era of industrialisation the world has seen over the last two hundred years.

Recently, though, there has been a trend on the principal stock exchanges in the world that more and more shares are finding their way into the hands of pension funds, mutual funds, hedge funds, insurance companies, etc. and less and less are held directly by individual members of the public. Stockbrokers have tended to reinforce this trend by concentrating their attention on their institutional clients at the expense of their private clients. This increasing institutionalisation of share ownership has the drawback of distancing the common people from the inner workings of the stock markets. It is as if they remain on the outskirts of the casino grounds while professional representatives gamble inside on their behalf and occasionally come out to brief them on how they, the professionals, are performing on the tables. This situation is not designed to make the casino model popular among the masses. It's not touchy-feely enough.

There is no reason why we should not revert to the earlier, more populist version of capitalism in South Africa. We simply have to widen the shareholder base. However, it does mean that individual members of the public must put up their own cash to participate in the new ventures being floated on the stock exchange. Yet that teaches the public the first important lesson of gambling: you have to put money on the table to win anything. Something never comes out of nothing!

This leads to the final point. A casino being open to all does not guarantee equality of outcome, i.e. that everyone who gambles in the casino will come out equal. Fate can be cruel. Some gamblers will win more than others. Some will lose, some will go bankrupt, but that is all part of the game. In fact, nothing is wrong with losing because it may turn the person into a better gambler (failure is the stepmother of invention). What the casino should guarantee is equality of opportunity, i.e. that everyone starts out with the same chance of success. After that, fate and the skill of the gambler will decide the outcome.

The slots are not enough

As one young entrepreneur who in the past had been barred from entering the casino as a result of apartheid said to me: "You should realise, Clem, that we're not just interested in playing the slots (one-armed bandits). We want access to the main gaming rooms as well and even to those small rooms where the really big punters play."

Right on! But it should be remembered that the big betters learnt the ropes with small bets and as their confidence and gambling skills grew, so they progressed into the bigger games. Without that crucial training period, anyone entering the small room (*le salon privé*) where the top punters play will be taken to the cleaners with no mercy. There's an old poker joke. If you look around the table and see no suckers there, the chances are that the sucker is you!

If you study the origin of most major league companies around the world in mining, industry and commerce, they began with a young entrepreneur with high hopes and a focused vision. The latest example is Microsoft, an American software computer company, whose founder Bill Gates was a teenage computer boffin. Its size now rivals IBM and he has become the wealthiest billionaire in the United States at a ridiculously young age. Nonetheless, one of the problems with the evolution of large companies is that when the founder dies, the person who inherits the mantle does not necessarily possess the same gambling skills as his predecessor. The successor may be well grounded in business administration, accounting, financial analysis, human resource affairs and industrial relations, but they are no substitute for a gambling instinct. It is an entirely different quality and as a result many outstanding entrepreneurs are terrible managers and vice versa.

The history of Europe, America and now Japan is littered with ill-conceived projects initiated by corporate leaders inexperienced in risk assessment. Yet history is also full of examples of companies that failed because their directors were so risk-averse that they would not dare change the direction of their companies in the face of overwhelming change. Frozen like rabbits in the headlights of a car, they foolishly stuck to the status quo. Of the top 100 companies in the US in 1956, only 29 were still in the top 100 in 1992.

There is no short cut to becoming a good gambler. You have to graduate from the school of hard knocks in the lesser games before you take on the big guys. This should, however, not deter any cocky young Davids from knocking an ageing complacent Goliath off the pedestal once they have acquired the knowledge and competence! It's been done before and it will be done again. There will always be a new kid on the block with more derring-do than sense in his head. He'll go for an outrageous gamble that he'll turn into a success by dint of hard effort and application. The drawback to getting older and wiser is that experience makes you think of all the risks involved in a decision. So you veto an idea which in your younger days you would have accepted gladly – and ensured that it worked.

Karl was no gambler

Karl Marx probably would not have appreciated the casino analogy because there is no evidence to suggest that he was a gambler himself. Still, he was correct in pointing out the problem of restricted ownership of capital, i.e. the few who have it and the masses who don't. As I have already stated, the casino must be all-inclusive. Thus, access to capital to purchase the chips to play on the casino's tables must be easily available to anyone who cares to gamble.

This does not mean that everyone will gamble with money. There are a whole host of people in society who for a variety of personal reasons wish to pursue different careers and lead different lives to that of an entrepreneur. Politicians and civil servants, teachers, doctors and nurses, trade unionists, missionaries, academics, social workers, housewives, editors and journalists, artists and poets, playwrights – all these people and more are driven by motives which have nothing to do with the impulse of gambling in a casino. All that society must do in their case is provide enabling mechanisms for them to switch should the gambling bug ever bite them.

The error that Marx made was to believe that profit was an illegitimate surplus. Profit is the winnings made out of the bet placed by an entrepreneur in opening up a business. Capital has to be put at risk for a return to be made on it. In a casino, as soon as the chip has been placed on the table the ownership of that chip goes into limbo. It is owned neither by the gambler nor by the casino. Only when the roulette wheel has stopped spinning or the dice have been thrown or the cards have been played does clarity of ownership re-appear. If the punter has won, his original chip is handed back to him, plus his winnings. If he has lost, the chip goes to the casino. In the real economy, it is slightly different. The entrepreneur's opposite number is the market. Either he gets his investment back plus a return or the market swallows up his investment.

Marx had an answer for this – take the uncertainty out of the casino by exercising absolute control over all the games played in it. By imposing perfect order, there would be no need for profit. The gamblers should stop gambling and work for the casino operator (the state) instead. This logic, however, ignores the fact that the most efficient way to create wealth is to give people the chance of winning on their own account. Marx wanted to take this excitement away, possibly because he himself was not acquainted with the neon lights, the green baize and the thrill of gambling. By making the casino a very boring place to be, he unwittingly sought to kill the goose that lays the golden egg!

Nobody has yet written the definitive essay on why, in the same decade of the collapse of the Soviet empire, many gigantic businesses in the world have turned in terribly disappointing results. I'm convinced that the roots of the failure in both cases lie in the way people are managed. As soon as too much control is exercised over their destiny, people cease to be creative. Employees are perfectly capable of being entrepreneurs in their work areas; they can be combined into smart teams which with inside knowledge can improve their work patterns far more effectively than management or outside consultants can. Given space, every employee becomes a gambler weighing up options, assessing risks and choosing the best course of action. Life under these circumstances is a lot more enriching than one hemmed in by central directives which allow no room to manoeuvre.

Modern Russia shows how difficult it is to reverse the ravages of central planning on the human mind. Emerging from 70 years of a totally grey existence, Russians are finding it painfully difficult to adjust to the fast pace and uncertainty of a free enterprise system. All that has happened so far is that a get-rich-quick mentality has nurtured a new class of racketeers and criminals who are dedicated to exploiting a population who for the most part are decent and forbearing but utterly bewildered by the changes. Russians are slow to rise to anger. However, if the provocation becomes too great, expect another mighty upheaval.

Good casinos encourage successful gamblers

Good casinos wanting successful gamblers may strike some as a contradiction in terms, since whenever a gambler wins, the casino loses (and vice versa). Obviously, in the longer term, casinos are like insurance companies: they have to make money out of their clients. But this should not stop the croupiers doing everything in their power to make the game easier for the players and working as hard as the players. Indeed, some players have to win spectacularly to keep others coming to the casino and to attract new clientele.

The economy in one important respect is different. Instead of the zero-sum situation of a casino where if one side wins the other side loses, it is win-win all the way. The more successful businesses are at making a profit, the more tax they pay. In addition, the more profit they make, the more they will invest in plant and machinery to make future profit and the more will be the number of employees who will pay tax on their wages. Equally, the more share prices improve as a result of improved profit and increased dividends, the more this will have a positive effect on consumer spending and therefore on value added tax. The bottom line is that the better business performs, the more government has to spend on good works.

It is therefore not surprising that an increasing number of politicians in many countries are rejecting the orthodox left-wing notion that entrepreneurs should only be accepted on sufferance. With the zeal of reborn believers in the notion of free enterprise, they have thrown their full weight behind business. It is as if the casino operators have finally decided not to sit in the back room and sneer at the customers behind their backs, but to walk around the tables, welcome the gamblers with open arms, congratulate them when they win and provide assistance where possible!

There has to be a dream machine

All gamblers want a shot at becoming millionaires. That's why national lotteries and football pools are so popular, the biggest individual win ever being $40 million from $35 worth of tickets in the Illinois State Lottery in 1984. It is also the reason for the best casinos having a slot machine that with the right pull will yield a jackpot of over R1 million. Often the "dream machine" is in effect a network of machines located in different casinos but linked to one another to allow the potential jackpot to rise faster than it could on a single machine. The equivalent in the real world can be provided to entrepreneurs by such entities as the European Union and the North American Free Trading Area which give a business the potential to launch a bright new idea on a much wider consumer base.

But the more important implication for economic policy to be derived from the powerful attraction of a huge prize, no matter how remote the chances of winning it, is the concept of unlimited upside. America has that quality in that a handful of dirt-poor youngsters in each generation end up being fabulously wealthy because they were in the right place at the right time to strike a chord with the American public. Nobody resents outright winners there as they do in more egalitarian societies like say Australia where there's a general dislike of "tall poppies". The disadvantage, though, of the American model is that quite a few top executives who have joined the "dream machine" bandwagon neither founded the company they're working for nor have turned in a creditable performance as the custodian of the existing operation. The only thing that relates them to the genuine rags-to-riches prototype is the king-size fortune they've managed to accumulate (without being inventive or successful). Their example unfortunately gives capitalism a bad name.

Nevertheless, fame and fortune have been, are and always will be very strong motivators for the remarkable few who make possibilities undreamt of by the more humdrum and mundane citizenry come true. Along the way, they usually make a significant contribution to society as well.

Rich casinos cannot afford to be surrounded by poor casinos

Arising out of the earlier points about casinos competing with one another and casinos being open to all, one problem above all others manifests itself. It is very difficult to run a casino with high-calibre staff and successful gamblers and keep them all secure if other casinos in the area are going bust with the consequence of high unemployment outside one's gates. The wall around the casino has to be very high indeed and supplemented by razor wire, fierce dogs and armed guards to stop intrusions.

Likewise, rich countries cannot afford to ignore their poor neighbours. Borders are always porous and refugees will always find a way of getting through if there is nothing to live for on the other side. Nationalism is a force for good and evil. If it is used to unite a country to become a "winning nation" economically or on the sports field, there's nothing wrong with that. However, if it is used as an excuse to prevent the creation of a wider economic area which includes the poorer brethren in the region or to discriminate against a particular group in one's own society, nationalism is exceedingly evil.

It's better to have a regional chain of casinos joined in the purpose of promoting "common wealth" than to isolate oneself from one's neighbours. Nationalistic rhetoric can be very seductive to the masses. Politicians indulging in it do so at their own peril, as regional conflict can be devastating. A member of one of my audiences wisely said the other day: "It's no good

gambling on a plush riverboat if it is heading for a waterfall!"
Selfishness gets one nowhere. Stingy nations never turn into
"winning nations".

Casino operators shouldn't get too close to the gamblers

If you were to see the casino operator being wined and dined
and earnestly engaged in conversation by one of the casino's
regular gamblers, you would immediately suspect that they
were cutting a special deal. Your conclusion would be that
whatever odds that gambler was getting when he laid his bets,
they would be more favourable than yours! Your assessment
might be right, it might be wrong (they might be just good
friends), but the inherent danger of such an incident in terms of
sending the wrong signals to all the other gamblers would be
there. Appearances can be deceptive but they matter.

Lobbying, where it is as obvious and heavy as it is in Wash-
ington, presents an unappealing image to the public. The feeling is that a great deal of money is exchanging hands – from
interest groups to lobbyists and perhaps to the lobby-ees as
well. In the process, no new wealth is being created. Quite to the
contrary, it is being dissipated on middlemen. Moreover, the
extra expense of having to lobby may be the straw that breaks
the camel's back for an entrepreneur keen on exploiting a new
market niche. Result: aborted mission, no project. "Crony capitalism" is a phrase that comes to mind. It was coined in England
in the 1960s to describe a relationship between government and
prominent business people that was just too cosy by half. Little
high street enterprises felt unloved and ignored.

Crony capitalism has been resurrected in a different and
more respectable form. This time around it's called the "German model". The emphasis in this model is not on lobbying by

middlemen to obtain a favour from the powers that be. Rather, the powers that be are a composite of the main interest groups. An alliance is struck between government, major business and the trade union movement. Decisions are taken by consensus, in contrast to the confrontational "British model" where a decision tends to be a compromise as a result of balancing the opposing interests of the three groups. The consensus model has extended itself into German business as well with the introduction of boards of directors that comprise both managerial and worker representatives. Much of the outstanding performance of the (West) German economy since the Second World War has been attributed to this model. Moreover, it is considered more in tune with the progressive ideals of a modern society in that it provides greater trade union participation at the highest level in both the political and industrial arena.

The strength of the "German model" is apparent when things go right and the economy is humming. When things go wrong, the weaknesses of the model appear. Old animosities between the three parties surface and because they are not accustomed to conflict with one another, unwise policy decisions are made which erode the competitiveness of the economy. Property developers go spectacularly bankrupt and some of Germany's star companies report staggering losses. But the real flaw of the model is revealed by this apocryphal story of a family visit to Sun City which includes Aunt Gertrude who came along for the ride.

Having spent the whole day entertaining the family with a trip around the game park, boating, swimming, et al., you're looking forward to a night on the tables. Your spouse is tired, the kids are tired but Aunt Gertie is not. So after supper, you offer to take her along to watch you play blackjack. The cards are going for you, the chips are piling up and all of a sudden she starts offering you advice. Because she's not a natural gambler, her advice is erratic; you sometimes take it, you sometimes don't. It muddles your own instincts and eventually you lose the lot. She's still as chirpy as can be since her personal finances are completely intact. The following morning she tells the family how surprised she is at how inconsistent you were. If it had been left to her, she would have won handsomely. The moral of this sad tale is: never listen to enthusiastic amateurs whose own money is not at stake!

But that's exactly what happens when the government and trade unions get in on the act of risky decision-taking in a commercial environment. Neither party is a specialist in this area; they have other agendas to follow, and if the "consensus" decision ends up as a complete fiasco, they will emerge unscathed and unblamed. The shareholders who put up the money carry the can, together with the workers whose jobs are jeopardised. The employers take the blame.

Leave gambling to the entrepreneurs, the operation of the casino to the government and the employees' interests to the union. By all means let there be frequent contact between the three, but don't let them exchange roles. They say that heaven is where the French are the chefs, the Germans are the engineers, the Italians are the lovers and the British are the police. Hell is where the British are the lovers, the Germans are the chefs, the French are the engineers and the Italians are the police!

The casino is open 24 hours a day

Cellular telephones, fax machines, pagers, Reuters screens, CNN and Sky TV, networks of personal computers linked in cyberspace – the paraphernalia of modern communications and information technology are changing work patterns dramatically. At the beginning of this century, business decisions were made on information which was hours, days or even weeks out of date, particularly when that information had to be transmitted across the oceans. In addition, people stopped doing business in the evening, had sundowners, went to the theatre or opera and generally switched off till the following morning.

Business used to be divided into daily episodes – now it is a continuum. As the world spins, the Tokyo and Hong Kong markets lead the way before one moves across to Europe and on to America. The dollar may rise against the other principal currencies in Tokyo, fall in London and rise again in New York. Gold may fluctuate in the same way. Or a fall in share prices starts in the West, gathers momentum in the East, which causes further shock waves in the West and so on. Whatever the pattern for each 24 hours in the currency, bond, share and "derivatives" markets, it has to be monitored closely and continuously. Otherwise, millions or even hundreds of millions of dollars, sterling, rand or any other currency for that matter can be lost through temporary lapses of attention.

The stress of maintaining a global watch on the markets with information being instantaneously fed from all parts of the globe on any financial statistic you care to name has led to many early burnouts. You have to be exceedingly tough to be a trader today in currencies or bonds or other instruments. The green baize of the gaming table has been replaced by the luminous green charts flickering on the rows and rows of the video display units in the trading rooms. The pandemonium caused by a "grand slam" win in the casino is repeated in the trading room when the market gets really hot. Phones ring everywhere, traders shout across the room, people crowd around the interesting screens. At other times, the room goes weirdly quiet with traders snapping their braces or twiddling their thumbs as they watch silent phones and engage each other in small talk over paper cups of coffee.

But the game never stops . . .

Economics and gambling don't yet mix

Perhaps it's because economists on the whole are not gamblers, but I have yet to see an economic model which reflects the day-to-day experiences of your average entrepreneur. Take classic supply-demand theory. This suggests that as demand increases for a product its price will rise, which in turn will call forth extra supply, which will then lead to another point of equilibrium in the market. Reality is far less neat.

There's a popular business game that is much closer to the truth. It involves the distribution of a particular brand of beer from supplier to wholesaler to retailer. No matter where this game is played, or by whom it is played, the sequence of events is always the same. To begin with, everything is in steady state – demand is steady and a sufficient quantity of beer flows through the distribution chain to satisfy the demand. Suddenly demand jumps because a popular rock 'n roll band uses this brand of beer as a prop in a video. The retailer increases its order somewhat from the wholesaler to cater for the growth in demand and the wholesaler does the same from the brewer. But then the shelves start emptying, panic sets in and the retailer substantially hikes its order which causes a similar reaction from the wholesaler vis-à-vis the brewer.

Consequently, an enormous avalanche of beer comes barrelling down the supply pipeline just as the increase in demand starts petering out because teenagers (who have a short memory) have moved on to another video featuring another rock band. The game ends with everyone absolutely up to their ears in beer.

The inevitability of this less than satisfactory outcome – even with the most competent of players – implies something fundamental is at work to produce irrational judgements. The answer is simple: everybody in the chain has incomplete information on which to base a decision at any moment in time. Of course, if they had consulted one another to obtain a clearer grasp of the bigger picture, they might have been more rational.

But in the real world it is never any better. Why do constrictions in roads cause traffic jams to form? The reason is that drivers don't slow down in a pre-planned and co-operative sequence ahead of a constriction. Information never flows that rapidly even with the latest tail-back warning systems. Besides, human beings are always at their most independent when behind the steering wheel. Nobody drives in unison with anybody else!

In business, a further motive stops any individual having perfect knowledge about the market. This is competition. No company worth its salt is going to tell its competitors about its future plans and strategies. Indeed it is trying to do the exact opposite – keep its decisions a closely guarded secret so that it can use the element of surprise to win extra market share, etc. This inevitably leads to boom-and-bust cycles where heightened demand for a product brings forth over-supply leading to surplus stocks, falling prices and reduced production until the position overshoots on the other side, and the cycle begins again. Surpluses and shortages, economic booms and recessions, bull and bear stock markets will always be with us. The herd instinct is strong when it comes to reacting to public news in the marketplace. If it's good, everybody rushes in; if it's bad, everyone runs for cover. Very few companies use even rudimentary game theory to play scenarios of their competitors' possible reactions to the various decisions they may make themselves. Of course, this is where an intellectual intervenes with the comment that markets are therefore wasteful and how much better it is if everybody is compelled to co-operate to iron out the cycles. Over the longer run, though, the chaos of capitalism has proved itself as a more effective force in creating wealth than the order imposed by socialism.

Even Keynes, probably the most prominent economist of the 20th Century, did not make allowances for the essential role that the gambling instinct plays in economic growth. He maintained that the best way to reverse a recession and alleviate unemployment was for the government to run a budget deficit and directly create jobs through state-initiated projects. The equivalent in the casino model would be as follows: to combat slackness of business, the casino operator decides to spruce up the interior of the casino using his existing labour force while adding former customers who have fallen on hard times to his payroll. The problem with this approach of creating artificial jobs is that it is not sustainable unless the casino's core business of gambling picks up. Otherwise, the house take eventually has to be raised considerably to fund the deficit or the casino goes bust. At best the Keynesian approach offers temporary relief: at worst it leaves the economy in worse shape in the longer run.

The technique today advocated by experts to get an economy back on track is the lowering of interest rates by central banks. Since the interest rate is the price of money from lenders to borrowers, the theory goes that by reducing the rate, entrepreneurs will find it easier to finance the projects they have in mind. The incentive to go ahead is that much stronger. Activity will pick up.

This method of stimulating economic activity certainly aligns itself more closely to the casino model. The equivalent is that the casino owner offers easy credit terms for gamblers to purchase the chips and play. The catch is that the casino's customers may, for any number of extraneous reasons, be pessimistic about their prospects. Hence, they don't take the bait, they stay away. Easy credit by itself may not generate the extra activity anticipated by the party that grants it. Or it may attract the wrong type of investors who bet on "white elephant" projects which don't add much to the overall level of output. Or it may precipitate additional consumer spending without the additional production capacity to meet it. In all these cases, easier credit merely raises the rate of inflation because more money is chasing the same number of goods.

All in all, future economic models should be less mechanistic, while addressing the psychology of the entrepreneur and the permanent uncertainty of the marketplace.

Gamblers help each other

The idea that all gamblers are cold-hearted and ruthless is a myth. Some are, but among the vast majority a camaraderie exists, such that if any one of them has a bad run the others rally round. The average gambler is like the James Garner of *Maverick* rather than the flint-eyed Lee van Cleef of *The Good, the Bad and the Ugly*. Regular poker-playing schools comprise friends who come together as much for the fun and the conversation as they do for the game of poker. Obviously, large casinos are more impersonal, but the respectable among them don't want to see any customer lose his shirt, his house and all his other possessions. However, it boils down to individual accountability – each gambler must know his own limits.

The best of big business behaves like a big-hearted gambler. It sets money aside for small business education and training. It looks internally at its in-house activities to see what can be subcontracted out to small business (and for good commercial reasons too). It provides finance to and acts as a mentor for new entrepreneurs to whom it has awarded contracts. It puts as much effort into social responsibility programmes and community initiatives to create jobs as it does into keeping its operations efficient. It believes passionately in creating an all-inclusive casino in which big and small gamblers alike have an equal chance of making a fortune.

The energy of the best of business can also be harnessed to assist government at national or provincial level to meet objectives they set in the fields of housing, education and health. A national lottery, for example, could be organised by the private sector with the proceeds going to welfare. It is a supreme irony in this country that the home construction business is operating at well below capacity, the building societies are flush with cash but the earnest desire of millions of people to get a job and own a house remains unsatisfied. A way to help can be found. Obviously, business wants to make money out of meeting the housing demand. But it also understands the necessity of maximising the number of new jobs created in the process. A casino operator with sufficient charisma and passion will always be able to touch the hearts of the gamblers and make them play in games where the pot goes to charity.

A casino is a closed system

It is a less than universally known truth that a casino is a closed system (not to be confused with a closed club). If the casino operator decides to encourage gamblers to play a particular game by offering better than usual odds, then to keep the casino solvent he has to make the odds more unfavourable elsewhere.

In the real economy, subsidies and tax incentives to one sector must in the same way mean levies and higher taxes on another sector. Politicians worldwide will stress the subsidies and tax incentives on account of the fact that they can be positive about them; but they'll silently pass over the concomitant levies and higher taxes because they don't want to spoil the good news with bad news. Paying Paul sounds so much better than robbing Peter!

The late Don Caldwell used to say in his inimitable way that when a government announces some new welfare scheme, the headline should not be "Government to spend R100 million on welfare". Rather it should be "Government announces tax increases of R100 million to finance new welfare programme". It doesn't sound so good if you present both sides of the equation.

One can easily commit the mistake with big systems of thinking of them as open-ended (or to use a more familiar expression, as bottomless pits). Economies, however, obey the well-known maxim of business: there is no such thing as a free lunch. No gain without pain!

A high house take encourages informal games

Should it become a widely held belief that the house take of casinos in a particular neighbourhood is unfairly high, gamblers will establish their own games – in doorways, on the streets, on benches in the park, in smoke-filled rooms in private houses and in basements of illegal casinos. Gamblers are reluctant to see too many of their resources absorbed on ancillaries. Beyond a certain point, they will rebel against the system, set up their own structures and do their own thing.

Taxpayers are no different. As taxes become more severe, energy is switched from creating wealth to tax evasion and avoidance. Legal loopholes and write-offs against tax are more enthusiastically sought (which is only good for the lawyers). Large parts of the economy go underground. Accounts are duplicated by owners of businesses. Official statistics of activity become less and less significant. Bartering of goods and services rockets as individuals eschew any exchange of cash which may attract tax. From the point of view of government, the most important consequence may be a fall-off in tax receipts. However efficient tax collection is, one must never underestimate the ingenuity of the man in the street to conceal his income and assets when he feels he is being unfairly penalised.

This section demonstrates that one of the critical characteristics of a good minister of finance is a sixth sense about the tolerable limits of tax.

Gambling is a great leveller

In any game of chance, the family background, class, colour and gender of the player are irrelevant. Educational qualifications are pretty much so too. Shrewdness should not be confused with education. The only thing that counts is the player's skill at gambling and the cash he or she brings to the table.

Cash resources can over-ride skill in a game such as poker where no limits apply. A rich, mediocre player can raise the stake on an individual hand to a level which forces a poor but skilful player to throw in his cards (as he can't risk the chance of ruin even if he feels he can win the hand). However, for the vast majority of games, and for poker where betting limits are agreed beforehand, a gambler's performance is heavily determined by skill – and luck, although Gary Player once said: "The more I practise, the luckier I get!"

Stories abound of young hustlers with few resources who have honed their skills at pool, backgammon, various card games, etc. and who then use these skills to fleece rich, unsuspecting opponents. Hollywood has glamorised "hustling" with the likes of Paul Newman, Robert Redford and Tom Cruise. America loves the kid who comes from nowhere to scoop the pool.

Business is as good a leveller as gambling. If it's jobs for pals at the top of a commercial organisation and the pals happen to be non-gamblers, the organisation will head one way – south! It is so easy for the top to lose touch with the game, particularly when the game is becoming more complex than when the top were young and played it themselves (as is now the case with the "derivatives" market). Being a well-mannered, handsome, articulate, charming, urbane aristocrat is no defence against a street-wise, lean and hungry entrepreneur. I know whom I'd put my money on.

Gambling is no sin

Among the intelligentsia, gambling is regarded as a fairly grubby activity undertaken by roués. But we all do it (not necessarily with money) because life from the day we're born is uncertain and messy – full of surprising twists and turns and constantly providing options from which we have to choose. As John Lennon sang to his son: "Life is what happens to you while you're busy making other plans." Madonna simply asserted: "I'm a gambler." Academic paths, jobs and careers, places to live, spouses, friends, business colleagues – the selection of the ones we find most suitable in each of these categories requires judgement in the face of incomplete evidence. Gambling is as natural and as essential as breathing.

In reality, no amount of analysis or foresight can stop the future from being uncertain. As a first principle, we have to accept uncertainty graciously. Hence, we ought to examine a range of possibilities. After all, it is better to be vaguely right than precisely wrong! Indeed, in the world of perception, we move from multiple pasts where historians argue over differing interpretations of what has been into multiple futures where experts provide conflicting prophecies of what will be. It is like walking along a misty mountain path which you do only once because life has no repetition. When you look back, you can recognise one or two familiar shapes that you have just passed. Further back, the path disappears into the mists of forgetfulness. Looking in front of you, the path is apparent for one or two paces ahead but thenceforward you have little idea where it leads, though fuzzy shapes offer you one or two suggestions.

I only have to look at my own life to support this thesis. If one of my Oxford friends had said to me in 1966 that I would one day wind up in South Africa looking after some gold mines, I would have said he was nuts. But in August 1966, I was on holiday in Cornwall recovering from my final exams when a chance event completely changed the rest of my life. I was needing someone to act as crew in a dinghy race one lunchtime in a place called

Rock on the north-western coast of Cornwall. The place is renowned for a pub which used to be frequented by smugglers, these lines having been written on the wall: "Them that ask no questions seldom tell no lies, so watch the wall my darling as the gentlemen go by." I invited a complete stranger sitting on the wall outside the pub to crew for me. She accepted. I subsequently met her father who worked for Anglo and that's how I joined the Corporation. Thereafter, through a series of unpredictable opportunities presenting themselves and personal choices I myself made, I am where I am. But none of this was known to me when I was 21. I'm sure there are many other people who have walked in a similarly random fashion through their lives, backing a hunch and taking a gamble whenever they were confronted by a fork in the path ahead.

In a funny way, South Africa's future from the time I gave my first "High Road" lectures in the middle of 1986 has demonstrated the same characteristic. I remember at the time saying "the future is not what it used to be". Well, it certainly wasn't. If I had outlined to my audiences then the future that actually transpired in South Africa from 1986 to 1994, nobody would have believed me. It makes one think that, although one can set an inspirational goal sometime in the future (in this case a negotiated political settlement), it is often unwise to describe in any detail all the incremental steps needed to reach the goal or the dates by which such steps should be achieved. Scenarios should be painted in vivid colours with a broad brush, like a late Turner masterpiece. In the first book I wrote, *The World and South Africa in the 1990s*, I made the following statement: "To launch people into the unknown and make them display exceptional courage – for that is what the 'High Road' entails – requires a common vision. The most critical part of this vision is to put all South Africans first." South Africa has taken the risk and reaped the reward. If that's not gambling, I don't know what is.

One business consultant long involved in strategic planning put it rather well: "Perhaps you should only plan for a 'next step' future. All further steps are options which can only be weighed up against one another when that step has been taken. The future has to be treated one step at a time." It is fanciful to adopt the approach that one storyteller did when he had written his hero into an impossible situation in a monthly episode in a magazine (the hero was totally surrounded and outnumbered by the villains). He started his next episode: "With one bound he was free . . ." Reality involves a series of less dramatic leaps over hurdles and fences as they arise. So far South Africa, like a thoroughbred, has cleared them all – and floored the cynics. But you'll never stop doom sayers predicting that the country will stumble at the next fence. We'll confound them yet.

I heard a marvellous science fiction story the other day which illustrates the law of unintended consequences that makes life even more accidental and uncertain. This law states that small causes can lead to overwhelming and sometimes unwelcome effects. A boy living today is offered a ride back in a time capsule by the inventor of the machine – along the lines of the movie *Back to the Future*. He asks to be taken back to the time of the dinosaurs so that he can photograph one of them. This is because in his current world no version of *Jurassic Park* exists! Back in time they both go and as the boy is about to step out of the craft, the inventor tells him not to veer off in any way from the path leading away from the craft. Off the boy goes and around the first corner he spots a dinosaur, photographs it and starts hurrying back to the craft. On his return journey, he sees this lovely flower and walks ever so slightly off the path to take a closer look. Satisfied, he returns to the path and arrives back at the craft. The inventor congratulates him on getting the photograph, but asks him whether he strictly obeyed the instruction. Shamefacedly, the boy says that he made the smallest detour to examine a flower. The inventor looks aghast and asks the boy to show him the soles of his shoes. Alas, on the sole of one shoe is a flattened butterfly that the boy stepped on by mistake. The inventor strikes his forehead with his hand and exclaims that this is an absolute tragedy, whereupon the boy asks why. The inventor says: "Wait till we get back to the

20th Century!" When they do arrive back, everything is out of kilter, including the fact that the society they live in is no longer a benevolent democracy but a malevolent dictatorship. The law of unintended consequences had struck back with a vengeance.

Samples of this law from real life abound. My favourite example is the one of the obscure Dutch lens-grinder Jan Lippershey, who on 2 October 1608 offered probably the first telescope ever made to the authorities in Holland. Within a few months, his invention had been replicated in Italy, which permitted Galileo to substantiate his belief that the earth orbited around the sun. There was no way the lens-grinder knew in advance that his invention would shortly lead to such an important scientific result. In the 18th Century, a similarly unpredictable chain of discovery was triggered by the invention of a steam-driven pump for the coal mines. This led to steam-driven looms which ushered in the Industrial Revolution in England, which in turn led to the steam locomotive that opened up America. Finally, steam drove the turbines to generate electricity. What a result from such a specific need to begin with! So often the later applications of an invention were never dreamt of by the inventor.

Another remarkable story was the way Alexander Fleming discovered penicillin in 1928. In a dish of cultures of staphylococcus bacteria, Fleming noticed an unusually clear area surrounding a spot where a bit of mould had fallen into the dish. He remembered that in 1922 he had prepared a similar dish of his own cold germs. A tear from his eye had accidentally fallen into the dish and created a similarly clear area. He had at the time come to the conclusion that his tear contained a substance which caused rapid destruction of the bacteria. He had named the antibiotic enzyme in the tear "lysozyme".

In his own words, he later related: "But for the previous experience with lysozyme, I would have thrown the plate away, as many bacteriologists have done before . . . Instead of casting out the contaminated culture with appropriate language, I made some investigations." He added: "There are thousands of different moulds and there are thousands of different bacteria,

44

and that chance which put the mould in the right spot at the right time was like winning the Irish Sweep."

But that's life – leaps in science usually arise from small observations or inventions that are opportunistically pursued. Contrarily, it is also known that modest interventions in ecosystems can lead to disastrous consequences for plant or animal life because of the complex inter-relationships of all the factors that make up the system. Hence, people these days are asked to think holistically about complete systems rather than in a focused manner about separate components.

The conclusion I've come to is this. We live in an imperfect world, the essence of which is uncertainty. Quantum physicists who have examined the subatomic world would agree with me. To define one pathway into the future by means of a forecast is therefore extremely dangerous, however brilliantly devised the forecast is. There are many things that can happen unexpectedly and by chance which can upset it. Moreover, many forecasts are not that brilliant because they merely reflect the wishes of the forecaster and, as we know, the future often turns out independently of our wishes. Think of all the "hockey stick" forecasts made by companies for their products' price and demand. A "hockey stick" is a forecast that is conservative in the short term but rises into the realms of never-never land in the long term. Wishful thinking ultimately gets the better of realism. It is therefore more prudent to view the future as a cone of uncertainty opening up the further one peers into it and then to examine feasible possibilities within the cone. One then must apply instinctive probabilities to those possibilities and then determine the best course of action. As the future unfolds, the probabilities may change and new possibilities will emerge, which can alter the course of action perceived to be best at any moment in time.

This is why I've advocated for the past eight years the idea of thinking in terms of multiple scenarios. It is far better to have a flexible mind set that adapts to change which is beyond one's control, than to have a rigid mind set (however brilliant the individual is) that can snap as a result of unexpected change.

Earthquakes occur when faults are brittle and only give way at the last possible moment. Huge amounts of energy are released and destruction occurs. The same is true of rigid thinking. When it is absolutely obvious that the opinion being held is wrong, panic sets in and stupid decisions are made under undue stress and strain.

In other words, take a simple piece of gambling advice: never bet the shop on a single outcome. Sure, you can strike it lucky by putting forward one hypothesis on the future and then being proved right. Some extremely successful businessmen have done just that. But it's a high-risk strategy and one that comes to grief more often than not, because wild cards can upset the whole pack. In the long run, the best strategists keep all their options open for as long as possible and accept a little less gain. They know when to quit a particular course of action and conserve their energy for other things that count. As I've already mentioned, there's nothing wrong with failure. Failure is often a pre-condition for success. Think of all the scientists who've gone up blind alleys before making a breakthrough. Think of all the authors who've persevered and written best sellers after their first draft has been rejected.

Nature itself understands the concept of being ready for any scenario that can be thrown at it. The incredibly rich diversity of plants and animals (as well as in many instances superabundance of offspring) is such that some species will always survive whatever changes happen in the external environment. One of the dangers of modern agriculture is that monoculture is taking over from diversity as farmers specialise in only the fastest growing crops with the highest yields. The meadows with a dazzling variety of wild flowers have made way for fields of single kinds of vegetables and cereals. The cutting down of the tropical forests means we're losing forever ten species of fauna and flora every day. By our intervention in nature, we're gradually betting on fewer and fewer species to take us into the future.

Gambling is no sin. It's what we do all the time. Moreover, resolute gamblers shrug off the loss of one spin of the wheel or one roll of the dice. One setback does not intimidate them. The tougher the game, the more resilient they become. I hope nature fights back!

A final story from my youth. At the conclusion of my first tutorial on philosophy at Oxford, I addressed the following enquiry to the legendary old philosopher who had been lecturing me: "Same time next week?" He responded: "That depends." "Depends on what?" I asked. "The way the intervening period unfolds," was his comment. "Really?" I said. Sensing my discomfort, he made this unforgettable retort: "You have just learnt the first lesson of philosophy: absolute answers don't exist. The difference between your young enquiring mind and my old experienced one is that you don't know, whereas I know I don't know."

Aces can be trumped

In bridge, aces can be trumped. In chess, as you are developing an intricate strategy, a bishop appears from nowhere and checkmates you. In horse-racing, the outsiders sometimes win. Professional gamblers are always on the watch for the peripheral scenario which might just eventuate and ruin their bet (or make them millionaires).

Peripheral vision is exemplified by deer or buck drinking at a waterhole whose ears prick up at any perceptible sound and who constantly look up from the water to scan the immediate neighbourhood for a predator. Horses acquire greater peripheral vision when they gallop in order not to stumble. Hence, some of them wear blinkers in a race. Animals reserve their sharpest instinct for when they are in a survival mode. For that matter, so do human beings. Have you gone for a walk in the woods or down an ill-lit street at night? Your senses become keener. You try to interpret any sound like the snapping of a twig or the rustling of a bush or footsteps on the pavement. Is it a threat or nothing to worry about? You look around to see if something is gaining on you.

But let me tell two stories about the absence of peripheral vision. The year is 1876. A young man walks into the head office of one of America's most successful companies of the pioneering period. Throughout the country their offices are linked by tens of thousands of miles of telegraph wire carrying countless messages in Morse code. They are looking to improve the system because one wire can only carry one message at a time. If they were to continue with current technology, they would be faced with the huge expense of multiplying the number of wires many times to cope with the expanding market. Their efforts are therefore focused on modifying the equipment so that several Morse code messages can be carried on a single wire simultaneously.

The young man says they're barking up the wrong tree, as he has invented a machine that can transmit voices. He offers to sell the patent for this machine to the company for $100 000. They say thanks, but no thanks, and instead opt to continue with the development of an expensive multiplex telegraph system. Two years later they realise their mistake and offer the young man $25 million for the patent rights. This time he turns them down as he has already started his own company. Thereafter he successfully challenges two of the company's subsidiaries for patent infringement. So, who are we talking about? Well, the company was Western Union, the young man Alexander Graham Bell, his invention the telephone and his own fledgling company Bell Telephone Company which became American Telephone and Telegraph.

A century later the most revered company in America invents a small intelligent box. Because it doesn't see this box as a threat to its core business of making large intelligent boxes, it decides to share the secrets of the inner workings of the small box with other people in the trade. A young man, together with his friend, enthusiastically takes up the challenge of putting together a similar, more user-friendly small box of his own in the family garage. In his own ambitious words it is going to make "a dent in the universe". He succeeds not in making a dent in the universe, but in precipitating a revolution in the intelligent box industry which strikes at the heart of the giant's core business, causing it to lose $8 billion in 1993. As you probably already have guessed, the giant is IBM, the young man Steve Jobs who, with his friend Steve Wozniak, launched the Macintosh personal computer in January 1984.

Two stories separated by more than 100 years, but with a remarkably common feature. Something small and seemingly irrelevant became deadly central very quickly. You could almost hear the management in the two companies saying to begin with: "Who is this young whipper-snapper that thinks he can upstage us with his invention?" But new technologies and sudden changes in fashion or values do just that – upstage the establishment and leave them twisting in the wind no matter how good their previous track record may have been. You are only as good as your last decision.

In particular, Western Union was besotted by a vision of the future full of customers sending millions of messages via Morse code and telegrams every day. It therefore ignored the fact that people would jump at the chance of communicating to one another through speech because they would feel closer together. Latterly, IBM focused on a future full of customers handling their data requirements through ever more efficient mainframes. It therefore missed the implication that the shift in values in society towards greater autonomy and freedom of the individual would inevitably lead to an exponential demand for personal computers, displacing the mainframe as the principal purveyor of information. Both Western Union and IBM saw the future like a single railway track heading out to the horizon, along which the train of events would travel their way. They perceived a "single desired future" – clearly and wrongly.

In ships and aeroplanes we add radar systems to our natural senses. Thereby potential hazards such as storms and other objects can be spotted earlier and further away. It would be considered utterly foolish if pilots of ships or planes looked straight ahead when making their journey through the seas or skies. Radar is therefore not focused in a narrow beam in the direction of travel but rather conducts an all-round 360 degree sweep. Indeed, in wartime, it is essential for ships to be on a permanent 360 degree lookout for incoming torpedoes; likewise planes for incoming missiles. It is therefore astonishing that in business the forecasting approach is so common, as it is equivalent to the captain switching off his radar system and going on a predetermined route irrespective of dangers lurking in the vicinity of the craft.

If you picture the future opening up as a cone of uncertainty, then it makes absolute sense to illuminate it with a broad beam of light and use every ounce of your imagination to dream up peripheral possibilities. It makes no sense to try and pinpoint the future with a single forecast. Have you ever tried tobogganing at midnight down a steep icy country road with only a small torchlight to show the way? I did it a few years ago in a snowy February in New Hampshire in the United States. There were three of us on the toboggan – Bruce Scott, a professor at Harvard Business School, Pierre Wack, ex-head of scenario planning at Royal Dutch Shell, and I. Three experienced futurists and one pencil-slim ray of light. We should have known better! We missed a critical bend at considerable speed and ended up in a snowdrift at the side of the road. A soft landing, thank heavens! But the methodology was suspect. Peripheral scans are essential, whatever your walk of life. Otherwise your ace may be trumped.

In South Africa's case, the peripheral event that could become absolutely and deadly central to our lives in five years' time is Aids. It appals me that the contemporary political and economic debate has relegated Aids, until very recently, to the middle pages of journals and newspapers. I seldom make hard predictions, but before the turn of the century it will be the headline story here – and we shall deeply regret our short-sightedness if we do not take advantage of the current window of opportunity to halt the spread of the epidemic by giving it as much publicity as was given to the 1994 election.

Kids should be taught to gamble

Recently I was talking at an elite, private high school and I made the following challenge to the pupils there. "You are probably only playing one scenario in your heads. Because yóu are being given a very good education, you believe you are guaranteed a job after leaving school or after you leave university after leaving school. Perhaps you should start imagining the alternative which is that no-one will offer you a job when you enter the world at large. It's happening to school children everywhere – in America, Europe, Australia. Serious-looking teachers hand you a piece of paper called a school certificate and later equally serious-looking professors confer on you another piece of paper called a degree. Yet when these pieces of paper are attached to your curriculum vitae and furnished to potential employers in the marketplace, you quickly learn that little value is given to them.

"Around one half of graduates of 1993 in any country you care to name haven't yet got a job in 1994. A story from Australia says it all. A doctor in Perth asked a plumber to mend his sink, which took the plumber ten minutes. The plumber presented a bill to the doctor for 200 Australian dollars. The doctor said this was monstrous. He only charged his patients 100 Australian dollars for ten minutes, to which the plumber replied: 'I know. I used to be a doctor!'

"The world of education and the real world of jobs are totally out of 'sync' with one another. The guarantee of a job is a myth. Moreover, the highly programmed, regimented world of being a school child ill-suits you for the uncertainty of life afterwards. The bell rings in the morning, you attend classes and listen to teachers as passive observers for set periods; exams come and go right on schedule; in those exams they ask precise questions which demand precise answers; during your career at school you climb the hierarchy from junior to senior and if lucky become a prefect – all these experiences intensify the belief that life proceeds down a single track from the past into the future.

Then, hey presto, you're dumped into this world where prospective futures are multiple, choices have to be made, risks have to be assessed and maybe you have to create a job rather than obtain one. It makes you think, doesn't it?"

Hopefully what I said turned on a light in the minds of the young audience. I know of only a handful of schools in South Africa which have addressed this problem seriously by establishing classes on how to become an entrepreneur. But talk and chalk can only go so far. Can you imagine trying to explain a game of poker to a kid without playing a few hands?

One school understands this and has gone for the much more hands-on approach of subcontracting some of the activities of the school to the pupils (in a commercial manner so the pupils are paid). The headmaster tells the delightful story of one pupil who came to him and asked for a franchise to sell Coca Cola in the school. This the headmaster granted and the pupil made R14 in the first week. So another pupil approached him and asked for the Coke franchise too. Again the headmaster said O.K., thus granting a second identical franchise in the same market. The first pupil immediately sought an audience with the headmaster and bitterly complained about this development. The headmaster responded by recommending to this pupil that he visited all the cafés in town to see how many sold Coke. The pupil returned after a reconnoitre of the cafés and said that all of them were selling Coke. "Yes," affirmed the headmaster, "and that's why you must accept competition."

A few weeks went by and the price of Coke started to rise suspiciously in the school. The headmaster called both pupils to his study and demanded to know whether they ever talked about the price of Coke, quotas, etc. They nodded their heads and innocently remarked that such topics came up as the last item of conversation at school break after sport and other things. The headmaster sternly admonished them. Any exchange of information about these topics was prohibited, he said, since an exchange like this would break the normal laws of competition. Immediately, the price of Coke on school property dived!

These two young boys probably learnt more about free enterprise from this actual experience than any number of lessons could have taught them. You don't teach a child to play cricket by teaching him how to keep score. You get him into the nets for practice and out on the field for the real thing. A point I often make in my talks is that the majority of kids should be taught the mathematics of gambling as opposed to algebra, trigonometry, differential calculus and so on. If they are going to open up their own businesses, they should really know about permutations and combinations, the calculation of probabilities and the percentage of personal wealth that it is sensible to wager at a given level of risk.

This is not to say that they shouldn't also be studying history, art, literature and the other subjects which make a well-rounded person. Business is about ethics as well as profit.

Gamblers keep opposites in mind

Keeping opposites in mind sounds like a formula for contradiction. But gamblers do it and so do we all in our daily lives, as you will see in some familiar examples which follow.

When you place a bet in a casino, you are playing two scenarios at the same time – "I'm going to win" and "I'm going to lose". Depending on how sophisticated you are as a mathematician, you will calculate the odds on these two scenarios before you put money on the table. In roulette, it's pretty obvious what the odds are if you go for red or black or if you go for individual numbers. But in some of the card games, the odds are harder to compute. Nevertheless, one principle holds true throughout all games: in weighing up the odds of the two scenarios, as a rational as opposed to an impulsive gambler you will wager less money on a possible outcome, the less attractive the odds are of its materialising.

For those who seldom or never play a game of chance for

money, let's switch from the casino to the road. On the main highway from Johannesburg to Pretoria, many drivers play two scenarios as they approach any of the numerous bridges that span the route: "There is a speed trap under that bridge", and: "There is no speed trap there". Then they look for indicators which provide a clue as to the relative probabilities of the two scenarios. If there's a cop car parked under the bridge on the other side of the highway, strike one for the "speed trap" scenario. If there are skid marks on the tarmac, possibly strike two because they may be yesterday's skid marks. If people coming the other way are flashing their lights, major strike three! All the time, these drivers are keeping opposite scenarios in mind and instinctively varying the probabilities they attach to them. This ultimately determines their speed as they go under the bridge. An important point to add here is that there is no way of knowing the real position – there is a speed trap, there isn't one – until one actually passes under the bridge. However brilliant the judgement of the driver preceding that event, an unanalysable core of uncertainty will always surround it until it is over. The same condition of course applies in a casino where certainty – of a win or a loss – only exists when the wheel comes to rest.

Another example of the same thought process occurs when we take out insurance. We weigh up the "calamity" scenario against "life as usual" and then decide on how much insurance we need. A further example is when we watch our favourite team playing soccer or rugby and vary the odds on whether they're going to win or lose (or draw) as the game progresses. And what about the moonstruck maiden pulling petals off the flower – he loves me, he loves me not! Perhaps the most close-to-home example I can provide was during the run-up to the 1994 election. We all played two scenarios: "peace at last" and "apocalypse now". Every 24 hours the odds changed, until finally the patience and jubilation of those queueing to cast their votes swung the odds irrevocably in favour of "peace at last".

I hope that by now I have convinced you that keeping opposites in mind is second nature to us. Being smart is not about producing a stunning conception of a single future which turns out to be correct. The idea of searching for a magic answer is false. But that's exactly what American textbooks on strategic planning teach us *ad nauseam*. Bring in a whole bunch of experts, analyse the market in which the company is operating to death, refine all the information and insights down to one set of parameters on which to base the plan and finally believe so passionately in the plan that no alternatives are considered. This is a recipe for disaster. For, poor subjective creatures that we are, if we are pushed to make a forecast we tend to forecast our desires. On the weekend before the election here, I went to a luncheon party where all the guests were asked for their estimate of the results. In retrospect, our estimates reflected the way each of us wanted the election to pan out.

History, however, demonstrates that our little gathering was not alone. In 1200 B.C., the citizens of Troy woke up one morning to find that the Greeks who had been besieging their city for years had gone. All they saw on the flat plain outside their city gates was a gigantic horse. They wanted to believe that this was a peace offering because they were sick of the hardships of war. Only one person said it was a trick and that there were soldiers inside the horse. The lady's name was Cassandra, but she had no chance against the "peaceful offering" scenario. She was right and Troy was razed to the ground. In 1633 Galileo was forced by the Inquisition to recant his statement that the earth moved round the sun. The Inquisitors felt that this opinion was a threat to the church's existence since it diminished the importance of man. For them the sun moved round the earth because they wanted it that way. In 1887 two scientists, Michelson and Morley, in a very precise experiment measured that the velocity of light was the same in all directions, i.e. both in the direction of the earth's orbit and at right angles to the orbit. The reaction of the scientific establishment to this counter-intuitive result was not as bad as the church's. However, since they had invested so much of their reputation in the hypothesis that light travelled through an immaterial substance called "ether", they were not about to give it up. They therefore proposed some weird and wonderful explanation that objects physically con-

55

tracted in their line of motion (the Lorentz-Fitzgerald contraction). It was left to a young scientist called Albert Einstein to turn the scientific establishment upside down in 1905 when he unveiled his special theory of relativity which did not try to explain but merely assumed that the velocity of light was the same in all directions. Accordingly, objects would appear shorter if they were moving in relation to the observer.

The lesson to be learnt is that, however intelligent we are, the future can cross our desires. It is therefore dangerous to confuse a forecast with a wish, a goal, a target, an objective. Nations have fought unwinnable wars on this basis. They have thought that they could keep empires going forever on this basis. Companies do their strategic planning using a favourable set of assumptions on this basis. They have kept dud projects going for too long and lost more money than they needed to on this basis. Scientists have gone on believing in outmoded theories and twisted the evidence on this basis. Love is unrequited on this basis! Whether it's the plain want of something very badly, resistance to change or fear of loss of face – all these motivations tend to warp one's judgements about the future. The right side of the brain vanquishes the left, emotion overcomes logic and a single forecast fuses with a single desire.

Thus, if you happen to be in business and see the organisation being tempted down the road of a "single desired future", purposefully play the opposite "bad news" scenario and see what implications it has for you and your team and how you can develop a resilient strategy to counter a bad turn in the market. Sometimes bad scenarios offer unthought-of opportunities to get ahead and – vice versa – good scenarios reveal serious impediments. Above all, don't be browbeaten by experts who offer you their middle-of-the-road consensus forecasts into thinking that your unorthodox scenarios are silly. As one wag put it, a group of experts frequently make a flock of sheep look like independent thinkers! Often the future turns out to be exactly what it oughtn't to be. Consensus can be a very dangerous thing, because everybody can be proved precisely wrong. And don't be put off by colleagues who demand that you should stop sitting on the fence and put your neck on the block. No-one says that a gambler is being indecisive when he is wisely weighing up the odds before wagering a stake in a game of chance. "Multiple futures" thinking is not a formula for vacillation and indecision.

Certainly, your neck must eventually go on the block – a decision has to be made – but only after going through the proper "on the one hand" and "on the other hand" multiple-futures process. If bosses plead for a "one-armed forecaster", it's usually a thin disguise for using hierarchy to get the forecast they want. I call them "binary bosses" because they only think in terms of "0" (wrong) or "1" (right). "Bayesian bosses" play the odds. The Chinese philosophy of the *yin* and the *yang* of nature – for every quality, there is an opposing quality – is closer to the truth than Western-style thinking where the proposition is either right or wrong. Life is a constant balancing of opposites, so there is nothing wrong with and no contradiction in keeping opposites in mind. It's the "both/and" not the "either/or" logic that prevails in the end. The future is never linear. Even the Delphic Oracle was ambivalent!

Good gamblers see patterns others don't

In a game of bridge, the top players win matches by interpreting the "shape" of the hands they have been dealt. Chess masters, unlike us mere mortals, study the evolving pattern on the entire chess board rather than the movement of individual pieces. In the Japanese game, *go*, players seek to capture their opponent's territory by out-manoeuvring them from all sides. The Chinese game of *mahjong* involves four players and 144 tiles in desperately complicated relationships.

In business, the way to steal a march on your competitors is to have a unique grasp of the interaction between all the forces influencing your market. Pierre Wack called the method by which you arrive at such an original insight the gentle art of re-perception. We often have opportunities and threats staring us in the face, but we perceive them in the wrong light and don't see their true significance. As Pierre would say, a poorly observed fact is a most dangerous thing. He himself was responsible for one of the finest examples of re-perception in the mid-1970s.

The oil market at the time was quite nervous, having experienced its first oil price shock when the price went from $3 a barrel in 1973 to $10 in 1974. Pierre felt that the moment was ripe for Shell Oil executives to perceive the market from a fresh perspective. So he built an alternative market model. He suggested the following logic. Let's reverse the normal laws of supply and demand in the case of oil. Instead of demand falling and supply rising as the oil price rises, let's suppose that demand rises and supply falls. What makes this hypothesis feasible? On the one hand, consumer nations cannot apply conservation measures that quickly. So even though they're paying more per barrel of oil, any growth in their economies must feed through to growth in oil demand – even in a rising price market. Technological change to diminish consumption of oil per unit of output, such as a more fuel-efficient motor car, doesn't happen overnight. On the other hand, many producer nations – particularly in the Middle East – not only have a desire to conserve their oil reserves but also have fixed annual income targets. In a rising price market, they will therefore have the tendency to reduce deliveries to the market. Pierre then theorised that the continuation of a rising demand curve in the second half of the 1970s, in combination with a falling supply curve, could – as the two curves closed in on one another – precipitate a second oil price shock.

He re-perceived the market as one entering a "zone of anxiety" in which the principle of "irresistible temptation" would apply, i.e. the tightening of the market would turn the Rotterdam spot traders temporarily into the main actors influencing the market and they would seize the opportunity to make as much money out of the position as possible. This re-perception turned out to be correct, and the oil price nearly tripled from

$13 in 1978 to $36 a barrel in the early 1980s. Such an event offered huge opportunities and threats to the business. But, as Pierre says, it is no good writing scenarios offering these kinds of re-perceptions if they don't enter the mind set (or microcosm as Pierre calls it) of the decision-makers and challenge their hidden prejudices and assumptions.

The world is changed not by people who are right but by people who can convince others they are right. That is why language is as important as content. Shell was prepared for the second oil price shock in 1978 because Pierre had carefully formulated his scenario in language that would resonate in the minds of his colleagues. What started out as a peripheral idea – plus $30 a barrel of oil – became a distinct possibility to Shell before it became reality. The event therefore came as no shock. Nor is it a surprise that Shell is currently at the top of the league table of oil giants because of the flexible thinking initiated by Pierre's work in the 1970s.

In business, therefore, it is essential to indulge at regular intervals not only in thinking about what may be coming at you from the edge of the universe but also in re-perceiving the nearby field of forces and events. If you want to alert your team to the possibility of close encounters of an extraordinary nature, if you want to shake them out of their "business as usual" rut, then you have to depict your fresh new perspective in a way that immediately gets their attention. It's no good being a Cassandra to whom nobody listens.

Good gamblers know their limits

In a casino, a gambler knows precisely what he can and what he cannot control. He controls the choice of game he wishes to play, the amount he bets on each occasion and the frequency with which he lays his bets. What he doesn't control are the rules of any game he decides to play, and the way the card falls or the dice roll or the wheel spins.

Alas, this degree of humility does not extend into the world of business and politics. Returning to Western Union and IBM, they were at their peak at the time of their misjudgements. Time and again the condition of being industry leader is a recipe for thinking one controls more than one actually controls – in Western Union's case it was the telecommunications market of the last century and in IBM's case the computer market of this century. The Ancient Greeks would have called it "hubris" leading to "nemesis". Nowadays we would simply say "pride comes before a fall".

From the early days of King Canute seeking to hold back the sea; to Britain's attempt to hang on to America towards the end of the 18th Century; to the declaration by the designer of the *Titanic* in 1912 that it was unsinkable; to America's military involvement in Vietnam; to the Hollywood studios' slowness in appreciating the potential of video for earning royalties on their old films; to Encyclopedia Britannica's blindness to CD-ROM; to Euro Disney's recent debacle in France: "hubris" lies only a little below the surface. Whether it's the sea or the market, or an enemy, if you're conceited enough to think you are more powerful than it is, it may eventually find you out.

All the precise analytical techniques and scientific "systems" punted in business schools these days, all the computer models which churn out countless projections on this or that trend in the market, all the consensus forecasts on the future arrived at by so-called experts and gurus seem to imply that we are better equipped these days to face the uncertainty of the future. It's actually a gigantic confidence trick, because it sucks us into a false sense of security that we know more than we can really know and that we shape more than we can really shape. The global market has become vastly more complex and interdependent than in previous eras such that the power, influence and foresight of individual actors on the global stage have diminished. Nations and companies can simply no longer be all-powerful in today's competitive environment. Politicians too would do well to note how autonomous world economic cycles have become before they make false claims about how their policies will create new jobs, etc. Power and prophecy have their limits.

We worry so often about things over which we have no control instead of concentrating our energy on those things which we do control, particularly in this day and age of a constant barrage of bad news by the media. Take a game of tennis, for instance. You know you have no control over the rules of the game or the size of the court – they are given. Nor can you control the fitness and experience of your opponent, the racket your opponent decides to use or the tactics that your opponent sets out to employ to defeat you. But what you can control is your own level of fitness and preparation, the quality of your own equipment and your own tactics, though they may be thwarted by your opponent's.

The same applies in business. There may be aspects of the market you're in, such as its structure and the demographic, social and technological forces that shape it, over which you have no control. You also cannot determine your competitor's cost structure, research and development programmes, production plans, new model launches, etc. What you do control are your own factors of production, your own unit cost, your own quality and your own marketing programme.

Moreover, in terms of what you do control, it is essential to identify the points of maximum leverage. This is where a little pressure can achieve spectacular results out of all proportion to the input. Such is the philosophy of karate and acupuncture. Action logs in a business are usually flawed in this respect, because they contain too many items and too many milestone dates. They offer no guide as to where energy should really be concentrated to achieve improvements.

A story from Ancient Greece illustrates the principle of leverage – heroically and tragically. After his defeat at the Battle of Marathon in 490 B.C. by the Greeks, King Darius of Persia began to collect together a vast army to exact revenge. Before he could go to war he died. His son, King Xerxes, continued the preparations and ten years later marched with two million men towards Athens and Sparta. But to get to Athens his army had to pass through very mountainous country. At one point it was necessary to go through a narrow pass called the Pass of Thermopylae. This consisted of a small path around steep cliffs with a precipitous drop to the sea on one side. Leonidas, King of the Spartans, correctly surmised that this was the place to make a stand with 7 000 men.

For three days in August 480 B.C. he held off the might of the Persian army because the pass was so narrow that only a few men could get by at a time. It was only when a Greek traitor called Ephialtes betrayed him, by leading the Persians via a secret path over the hills behind the cliffs so that they could attack the Spartan force from the other side of the pass, that sheer numbers and military might won out. Even so, Leonidas, after dispatching most of his troops south to safety, held out on a hillock with 300 Spartans till every single man had been cut down. As was their custom, the Spartans had combed their long hair and decked it out because they knew they were going to die. The Greeks put a stone on the spot where the Spartans fell. On it were carved these words: "Go tell the Spartans, thou that passes by, That here obedient to their laws we lie." At the outset Leonidas was outnumbered by around 300 to one, but he carefully selected a site where the courage and toughness of his men – factors within his control – could be exploited to maximum effect. Giants in big business can similarly be defeated or even slain by chief executives of small businesses who discover the commercial equivalent to the Pass of Thermopylae.

A good example of leverage in a negative sense is the loss of your car key when you have parked your car in some remote location. If your car is equipped with sophisticated immobilisers and alarms, it becomes a useless lump of metal without that tiny object called a key. The frustration is immense. No doubt that's why "key" is synonymous with "leverage" when one talks of "the key to success", etc.

One place where leverage will count a great deal is in the future budget of the South African government. Given the already high percentage that government expenditure bears to total GNP (around 35 per cent), it is incumbent on those looking after the budget of each government department to go for maximum bang for the buck. For instance, in respect of housing and small business development, the cash is available in the private sector to provide small housing loans on the one hand and small business loans on the other. The bottleneck is caused by the additional risk usually associated with these loans. If the government were to provide certain indemnities in both cases, huge amounts of money could be released by building societies and banks to satisfy the twin objectives of creating homes and jobs. The government would merely have to fork out cash in the event of bad debts qualifying for state compensation in terms of the indemnities given. This would be a fraction of the cost of government trying to fund the programmes itself.

One should make the final point that not everything over which one exerts control should necessarily change. Many successful institutions have lasted for hundreds of years because they have not compromised on features which have evergreen appeal. For example, there are schools in England like King's School, Canterbury, which is more than a thousand years old, and Winchester College, which recently celebrated its 600th anniversary – both of them are still going strong and have no problem in attracting pupils. Indeed, part of their appeal is their tradition and history. The same would apply to many of the colleges at Oxford and Cambridge. Then there is the American Constitution. For a much shorter time frame, one can think of successful consumer brands in both England and America. For a much longer time frame, one can think of Christianity and Islam, Hinduism and Buddhism! Hence, in pursuit of the general principle of adapting to change, one must not throw out the baby with the bathwater by trying to revolutionise everything. In any institution, constitution, whatever, certain things should change and certain things should stay the same. The trick is deciding which.

Gamblers spread their bets

Watching seasoned gamblers playing roulette, one notices that when they place their bets on the table, they spread their chips around in a combination of bets. Investment funds do exactly the same. Not only do they seek an optimum combination of shares, bonds, commodities and currencies, but within each of these investment categories they hold a variety as well. Certainly this strategy won't win as much as the punter who puts all his money on the roulette number that wins or into the investment that shows the highest level of appreciation over the year; but then he is taking a much higher risk.

Gambling is all about hedging your bets to obtain the highest yield for a given level of risk that you find acceptable. Each gambler, each investor, has a different attitude to risk – some more conservative, some more daring – which alters the manner in which the chips are put on the table or the portfolio of shares is acquired. *"Chacun à son goût"* as the French would say (every man to his taste). I know of some people who stick to the simple formula for distributing their assets of one third in land, one third in shares and one third in cash. However, I also have an eccentric friend who was a horologist and put all his money for a time into purchasing antique clocks and made a fortune. It is possible with real expertise to narrow the range of your portfolio down to your field of expertise without substantially increasing the risk. But you have to know your onions!

Without going into the mathematics of portfolio theory, one can illustrate the advantages of diversification by contrasting a portfolio made up of a single investment in one company amounting to R500 million and one consisting of investments in 500 companies amounting to R1 million each. Imagine each investment is represented by a pendulum, and variations from the expected return are equivalent to the oscillations of the pendulum on either side of the central point. If 500 pendulums are swinging independently of one another and a random snapshot is taken of them, the average of their positions is likely to be fairly central, because the ones pictured on the left will be more or less counterbalanced by the ones pictured on the right. In fact, there is a fundamental statistical law which says that the average deviation from the central point is inversely proportional to the square root of the number of pendulums (providing they are independent). Quite the contrary result may therefore be obtained with a random snapshot of a single swinging pendulum: it may well be caught near the extreme point of its oscillation.

The point of this analogy is to show that, all things being equal, one is considerably more likely to achieve the aggregate return expected from a group of small investments than the forecast return from one large investment. Nevertheless, the condition of independence or zero correlation is seldom met in real life, many investments being positively correlated to a certain extent. For example, for investments all in the same country, their success/failure is partially determined by the state of the domestic economy. Positive correlation can be pictured by assuming that the 500 pendulums are joined together by a rod which makes them all oscillate in unison. Negative correlation, on the other hand, would be where the pendulums were linked to each other by springs and were set in motion in a counter-cyclical fashion. A snapshot taken at any time would then indicate that their average position was the central point.

It therefore normally pays individual investors to diversify their private assets into investments with as low positive correlation as possible and ideally ones with negative correlation as well. Gold for many years has been thought of as a precious metal coming close to the negative correlation ideal, on account of the widely held perception that it is a safe haven when financial markets are in a panic. In this fast changing world, one American investment guru recently gave the following advice to his clients in his newsletter (and remember this is to Americans!): acquire multiple income-earning skills (the average American has seven different jobs in his lifetime) and hold multiple passports, multiple currencies and multiple properties in multiple countries! I only qualify in multiple skills in the sense that if the gold price plummets to levels unknown in the next few years, I can go back to playing the guitar in a restaurant in Cape Town.

Companies, for the same motives as individuals, like to have a balanced portfolio of activities which is as far as possible recession-proof. One needs "stars" to balance the "dogs". Countries are considered fortunate if their industries are sufficiently widely dispersed that their export earnings and GNP growth are not too badly affected by a downturn in the global economy.

Lastly, one must draw a distinction between diversification and distraction. While a good gambler hedges his bets, he is never distracted from the game he is playing. Unlike the movies which picture the successful gambler with a glass of champagne in his hand and giving a running commentary on the game to the beautiful women that surround him, the real professional doesn't allow his concentration to wander for one second. I remember going to Loftus Versfeld with two of my friends who were keen backgammon players to watch the heavyweight bout between John Tate and Gerrie Coetzee. I sat between my friends with the backgammon board on my lap whilst they played during the bout. Not even the boxing distracted them.

In business, there is a major difference between a company which over time builds up a diversified stable of activities consistent with the skills and strengths it has at its core, and one that acquires a portfolio of businesses it knows little about and which perform badly because a distracted management cannot give them enough individual attention. The word "conglomerate" is normally reserved for the latter.

If there's no other way, gamblers go for the long shot

Having explained in the last section how risk-averse good gamblers are and how therefore they like to spread the risk, I must highlight one contrary quality. If their backs are to the wall and they calculate that only one high-risk strategy is available to them to win the game, they'll go for it. Miraculously often, the long shot pays off. They're like Columbo in the American detective series who on the tiniest shred of evidence and the remotest of outside chances pursues a line of reasoning which pins the crime on the most unlikely of culprits. Remember how he walks out of a room, stops and turns with his finger across his lips as if he has just recalled some minor inconsistency in the conversation he has had!

This type of thinking which involves never giving up even when the odds are stacked dramatically against you, but instead coolly reflecting on whether there are any tactics which can overturn the result, was borne out in a singular experience I had in 1970. I was having a quick beer and sandwich in a pub in the City of London during a lunch break from the office, and as is customary in the pub struck up a conversation with a complete stranger next to me. Somehow the topic turned to the game of bridge and he offered to bring his brother along to play my wife and me at our flat in Putney.

On the appointed evening, he duly arrived with his brother and after dinner we sat down to play contract bridge. I asked what stakes they played and he said: "Three pence a hundred or five pounds a hundred – take your pick." I thought this quite a strange response and opted for the three-pence game. As the evening progressed, it became clear that not only was their system of bidding something which neither my wife nor I had ever come across, but they also won hands from almost impossible positions. At the conclusion of the game, with the cards having been fairly neutral to both sides, they were 10 000 points up. I and my wife would have lost £500 each if I had chosen the higher stake! Obviously, I was intrigued enough by the result – we weren't that bad at bridge ourselves – to enquire of the two brothers how much competitive bridge they had actually played. At this point, the brother I had met in the pub revealed that they were Britain's number one pair and they occasionally liked to go out and play social bridge. No wonder then about the lopsided nature of the result!

Before parting, I asked them one question: "What are the key differences between an outstanding and an average bridge player?" The answer was that the outstanding player is the one who can manufacture a winning strategy out of lousy cards – virtually any game can be saved if one is sufficiently creative. Moreover, a really good player is patient, keeping his best cards close to his chest until the last possible moment. Like the big cats stalking their prey, who wait for their intended victims to browse a little too close before pouncing, the experts never make a move too early. In fact, one of the most pleasing tactics in bridge is to "squeeze" one's opponents out of their winning cards as the final tricks are played.

A bet is a bet is a bet

Simply put, the reasoning behind a R10 bet made by a gambler in a casino ought to be the same as a R1 000 bet made by a first-time entrepreneur in setting up his own business and a R10 billion bet made by a big business in going ahead with a major project. The high priests of "high finance" – the corporate financiers and the merchant bankers – like to invest tremendous mystique in their trade, just as the ancient Egyptian astronomers drew an impenetrable veil of secrecy over the formulation of the calendar.

But the three questions which have to be answered to judge whether a bet is worthwhile are universally relevant. What is the risk? What is the reward? Given the ratio of risk to reward, what percentage of my assets am I prepared to put into play? The analytical techniques to answer these three questions can vary from the simple to the amazingly complex, yet they all have one thing in common. They will never give a perfect answer.

It reminds me of Latin and Greek "unseens" we did at school; these were pieces of classical prose or verse which we had to translate into English unprepared. Inevitably there were words or phrases which one didn't know and which required a flight of fancy if the translation was to be complete. Nevertheless, one took cognisance of the surrounding context of the expressions one was having difficulty with to make an educated guess. The Duke of Wellington, who defeated Napoleon at Waterloo in 1815, once commented: "All the business of war, and indeed all the business of life, is to endeavour to find out what you don't know from what you do; that's what I call guessing what's on the other side of the hill."

In a similar vein, the ultimate judgement as to whether to gamble or not to gamble will rest on a combination of information and statistics, common sense, intuitive flair and faith. The result of the gamble will have an extra ingredient: luck. However, the difference between a successful gambler and a lucky gambler is that through applying the three-step methodology described above in a disciplined manner, the successful gambler will establish a more consistent record of winning. Not only will the occasions he wins outnumber the occasions he loses over an extended period of time, he will also – through added caution – do better on the big bets than the small ones. He will certainly not behave like the man who recently saved up $150 000 and went to a casino and was given permission to put it all on one spin of the roulette wheel. He put it on "red". "Red" won and he doubled his savings and walked out of the casino never to return! Professional gamblers seldom if ever take that kind of risk.

Before I'd even heard of scenario planning, I was fascinated by the rules of betting in business. I used to lecture at Wits

Business School in the late 1970s on a course specially designed for mining people, the topic being "the financial evaluation and financing of projects". I even wrote the lectures up in a manual which was quite widely distributed in the industry. My intention was to overcome the lack of formal training in the field and to trace from grassroots the methods used to evaluate a new gold mine. I wanted to show that the decision to sink a shaft system up to four kilometres deep with horizontal haulages radiating out from it to a reef that is often no wider than a human hand requires a gambling instinct you will rarely find among humanity. This country almost takes for granted the special courage – from owners and workers alike – that has been needed to extract 45 000 tons of gold out of the 120 000 tons mined to date the world over. In a few thousand years' time, people will gaze at our old workings in wonder and ask themselves what kind of heroic breed were those miners who chased the yellow metal down and down – into the very place inhabited by Old Nick and his mischievous gnomes.

Gamblers like to narrow the odds

This section deals with the first universal issue to be addressed in making a bet: the level of risk.

If you are a racegoer and in the paddock surveying the horses before the next race, likely as not you're looking for information that will assist you in any bet you lay. Put the other way round, you're trying to narrow the odds of losing. In pursuit of this objective, you search for yardsticks which improve your judgement of the relative merits of each horse; one of the obvious indicators being the look of the horse immediately before it is led to the start. In addition, you may have a form book which offers you a guide to the previous race history of each runner: whether it won in dry or wet conditions; whether it is a sprinter or a stayer over a long distance; and whether it has previously beaten other horses in the present race. You will also note the names of the jockey, the trainer and owner because their skills may add to or subtract from a horse's performance. You may be carrying a newspaper as well to see what the tipsters' selections are. Then again somebody at the course itself may be offering you an insider's hot tip.

You will assimilate all this information and compare it with the odds being offered by the bookies on each runner. Then you do two things which are equally important. You discard certain possibilities either because you don't think those horses will win (or be placed) or because you think the odds being offered do not adequately reflect the risk. With the remaining runners, you make the final selection of the one (or ones) you wish to back, either because you genuinely believe that that horse is going to win, or because the odds are so good that the horse is worth a punt. What you are unlikely to do as a veteran of the races is put money on a horse because you fancy its name or you're attracted to the colours that the jockey is wearing or you know the owners so you're making the bet out of sentimentality (you might put a small amount on for the last reason!). This is irrelevant information which will only sway amateurs attending the races who are out to have fun and a bit of a flutter. If, by contrast, you're in deadly earnest about "the sport of kings" you will be guided solely by form, the weights being carried and the odds.

Let's turn to another appropriate example. You have four boxes in front of you containing two coins. The odds on correctly predicting which box or boxes the two coins are in (they might be in the same box or in different boxes) are one in sixteen. For each box that the first coin is in, the second might also be in any one of the four boxes, making the total number of options four times four, which equals sixteen. If, however, you glean the information that two of the boxes contain no coins, the possibilities are reduced to four, thus quadrupling your chances of being right (incidentally showing the exponential value of information – by halving the boxes, you've quartered the options). If, however, you had been told that one coin was silver and the other gold, you would have been no better off from the point of view of selecting their correct location. That information would have been useless "noise".

Matches is a game played after golf in the bar. Each player is given three matches which he holds behind his back. He then puts a clenched hand on the table holding no, one, two or three matches. Nobody can see what anyone else is holding and the objective of the game is to forecast the total number of all the matches held in people's hands on the table. Whoever guesses right scoops the pool of money contributed by all players. Experience in playing this game demonstrates that the later callers have the best chance of victory because they can use the information from the earlier calls to exclude certain possible totals. They can narrow down the range (but because a player is not allowed to choose a number already quoted they may be pipped at the post by a lucky early call).

In all these examples, the value of relevant information is highlighted. This brings us to what should be the underlying reason for any feasibility study into any project. It is to examine all the parameters that might impinge on the rewards of that project and try to reduce the risk of undertaking it by cordoning off the probable from the improbable range of each parameter. You may well find when you do the sums that within the probability range of all parameters it is not worth proceeding with the project. But as was mentioned earlier on in this section, a negative decision is as important as a positive one. What you have to be on your guard for when reading a feasibility study are the purple patches of prose extolling the beauty of the selected project site, etc. which have nothing to do with the financial return. There may be reams of computer printouts which look businesslike and important but on closer inspection are utter "noise". Actually words written in computer print are like words spoken on TV. Credibility is automatically given to content even though it is often GIGO – garbage in, garbage out. Thus beware of feasibility studies in thick volumes that are hard to lift, let alone read. When sifting through detail, a simple maxim for distinguishing between what is and what is not of value applies: "Relevant information reduces the number of possible outcomes, irrelevant information doesn't." It is a fact of life that scarcely any projects possess the happy feature of appearing to be so profitable that losses are inconceivable whatever happens. Most straddle the thin line between success and failure, making improved knowledge crucial.

From my own field of gold mining, I shall describe the intricate thought process one goes through before laying a bet on a new mine. The starting point is the ore body – the *raison d'être* for the project. One has to estimate the size of the ore body, measured in millions of tons, and its grade, measured in parts per million or grams per ton, from cores measured in kilograms obtained from boreholes that intersect the reef. Drilling is therefore the supreme test of drawing general conclusions from a tiny sample. At R5 million for a fairly deep borehole plus deflections, there is a limit to the number of boreholes you can drill to obtain sufficient information about the structure and content of the ore body (including faulting and dykes). Nevertheless, statistical methods exist to tell one how closely spaced the grid of boreholes on the prospective mining lease should be.

Thereafter, if the provisional estimate of gold in the ground looks promising, one has to prepare an estimate of the capital expenditure required to establish the mine. This not only means itemising all the work that has to be done and putting a price to it in today's terms, it also entails applying cost escalation factors to all the work as it is scheduled over the construction period. Finally one adds a contingency sum which varies according to the accuracy of the estimate. To illustrate the kind of error that can creep into this step of the feasibility study, the "Chunnel", which is the undersea link that has just opened between Britain and France, is now anticipated to cost £10 billion compared to the original estimate of £5 billion.

The third step is an estimate of the annual working costs plus ongoing capital expenditure to run the mine, which can be obtained by examining similar shafts elsewhere which are actually in production. The hard part is applying a cost escalation factor to these costs where one is having to take a 25 to 30 year view of inflation. In effect, one takes today's inflation rate, adds a bit to be conservative and compounds expenditure at this higher rate over the life of the mine. At the end of the life of the mine, the costs of rehabilitating the site have to be figured in as well.

The fourth step, having located the shaft in the lease area and taken into account the probable dilution of the in-situ grade of the ore body during the course of mining it, is to calculate losses of gold underground and in the plant as the rock is blasted, trammed, hoisted and treated. Then one has the basis to work out a profile of gold production. This is normally shaped like a dome as production is built up to full capacity, held for a time as the sweetest grades are mined and then projected to decline as the shaft matures.

The fifth and hardest step of all is to make a realistic estimate of the gold price from the day the mine comes into production in five years' time to the day it closes 25 to 30 years later. It's difficult enough giving a range for the gold price for the next month or the next year, let alone looking many years ahead. Again, to be conservative, one tends to use a starting price below today's price and escalate it more slowly than costs. Moreover, it is usual to test the viability of the mine for a whole range of price projections (which are a combination of a dollar gold price and a R/$ exchange rate!).

Finally, with all this data, one does the financial runs to calculate the possible returns on the initial investment. Since the latter can be anything up to several billions of rand, the whole exercise can be considered as a gigantic leap of faith tempered by rational estimates and reasonable research. Remember, too, that I have ignored political risk as I am an optimist about the future of South Africa. As stated earlier in the book, it makes no sense for a government to risk taxpayers' money on a venture like this. Leave gambling to the gamblers.

Cash is king

This section deals with the second universal issue to be addressed in making a bet: the size of the reward.

Why does a shop offer a customer a discount for cash? It is a deduction from the face value of the article because the shop is getting the customer's money sooner than if it had granted him credit for the purchase. The shop can put the money to use in the interim period. This shows that the value of a cash receipt depends not only on the amount involved but also on the date when it is paid.

For gamblers in a casino, the time value of money is irrelevant because they are immediately paid out when they cash in their chips. If the casino offered them a series of postdated cheques, they would become extremely angry. Yet this is exactly what plenty of competition and lottery prizes do. They pay out, say, R1 million over twenty years at R50 000 per annum. Under these circumstances, any discerning gambler will determine the present value of such a prize, i.e. the lump sum of equivalent worth he could be paid now. The latter will always be less than the face value of the prize because cash now is a lot better than cash in the future for either of two reasons – it can be invested immediately to earn a financial return or it can be spent immediately to avoid inflation. For example, suppose inflation is projected to average 10 per cent per annum over the next twenty years. The aforementioned "R1 million" prize is the same as being given R425 678 now to blow on a shopping spree at Sandton City. In business jargon, R50 000 per annum over twenty years has a "present value" of R425 678 at a "discount rate" of 10 per cent.

For entrepreneurs, the concept of time value of money is critical. Continuing with the case of a new gold mine, one spends money from years 1 to 5 constructing the mine, and it is only from years 6 to 31 that the money rolls in to pay for the initial capital investment and make a return on it. If the prospective cash flows when the mine is in operation are less than what can be earned by keeping the capital on deposit at the bank, then one will definitely forgo the idea of the mine. Even if the returns are identical, one will still keep one's money in the bank because it's much less risky than a new mine. In other words, it's only if the prospective cash flows from the mine offer a rate of interest well in excess of a bank deposit that one will be tempted to make the gamble. Incidentally, to use business jargon again, the estimated post-tax rate of interest on a project is called either its "internal rate of return" or its "discounted cash flow yield" ("IRR" or "DCF yield" for short).

To sum up, then, the reward for a bet is either cash now (as in a casino) or cash in the future (as in business). If it is cash in the future, the timing of each receipt is as important as the amount. Incidentally, the "payback period" of a project, i.e. the number of years it takes to pay off the initial investment in pure cash terms, is a really useful statistic. The shorter the "payback period" the more likely one is to proceed, because once the money wagered is recovered, all profits thereafter can be considered a surplus.

For every bet there's an opportunity cost

It is a truism that wherever options exist, there must be an alternative forgone to the decision actually taken. The reward associated with that alternative (or with the next best alternative if there's a range of alternatives) is the opportunity cost. They say that when a man marries a woman, within a month he will find out whom she really wanted to marry – in other words her opportunity cost!

In gambling and in business where the financial resources of the decision-makers are limited, assessing the opportunity cost of any decision before it is taken is essential. When you're sitting on a good hand in poker, you can either adopt the approach of gradually raising the pot so that everyone comes along for the ride or you can significantly raise the pot in the first round in the hope that others but not everybody may be tempted to see if you're bluffing. These are mutually exclusive strategies, each with its own reward. One is the opportunity cost of the other.

For a project, allowance can be given to the next best alternative by making its financial return the hurdle rate which the project under consideration must exceed (assuming that the two projects carry an equivalent risk). If it doesn't do so, one can revert to the next best alternative. A more familiar example of how the principle of opportunity cost operates may be found in the choice of a portfolio of shares and bonds. Each share and each bond in the stock and bond markets has associated with it a combination of risk and potential return. A shrewd investment strategy is to rank not only the shares/bonds you have in your portfolio in terms of preference, but also those you do not have that are just knocking on the door. In this way, you are constantly reminding yourself of the opportunity cost of your existing holdings.

Notwithstanding how simple and obvious all this sounds, so often project teams get a momentum of their own and because their livelihood is at stake put the case for their project so persuasively to the company's board that opportunity cost goes out the window. The consequence of excluding other projects in the pipeline is temporarily forgotten. Equally, where people believe they have access to a bottomless pit of finance, there's no compunction on them to prioritise their proposals for expenditure since they are convinced that every one of them can be paid for. Opportunity cost is thus an alien concept to politicians of a generous disposition!

A friend of mine told me the other day what his most memorable opportunity cost was. In 1977 he bought a holiday home in Onrus, near Hermanus on the Western Cape coast. He paid R30 000 for it. He recalled at the time that he was thinking of buying Rembrandt shares but instead he bought the house. Recently he sold the house for R315 000, or R285 000 more than he had paid for it seventeen years earlier. He had no regrets in buying the house as opposed to the shares in light of all the pleasure it had given him and his family over the years (and the handsome profit he made out of it). For his own edification, though, he calculated what the Rembrandt shares he had forgone were worth today: several million rand. Somehow, the opportunity cost made those holidays seem a little more expensive!

Another story with the same twist was of the man who was playing the dream machine at Sun City. Because he did not want to lose his place, he left his son with some coins to continue to play the machine while he went to obtain more change. The son put in three coins, pulled the handle and promptly won a jackpot of R120 000. If he had put in five coins it would have been the jackpot of over R1 million. I'm sure the father doesn't recollect the prize of R120 000 half as much as the opportunity cost of losing R1 million by not being there for the next pull.

The classic tale of opportunity cost is the parable of the talents in Matthew. A landowner who went away on a journey entrusted one of his servants with five talents of money, to another he gave two talents and to the third one talent. When he returned, he found that the first two had put their talents to good use and doubled them while the third, fearing his master's wrath, had hidden his talent in the ground. The first two were congratulated, whereas the third was castigated because he could have at least put the money in the bank and earned interest. Woe betide anyone who keeps his money under the mattress. There could be wailing and gnashing of teeth because of the interest forgone!

Every gambler has a misery curve

This section deals with the third and final universal question anyone should contemplate before placing a bet: given my assessment of the risk and reward of the proposition in front of me, how much of my wealth am I prepared to lay on the table?

The solution to this problem lies in determining your own "misery curve", i.e. how much pain you feel at various levels of loss. You might say this is painting a pretty dismal picture of the gambling process – what about the "happiness curve"? But life is asymmetrical. We can wipe out the planet with nuclear bombs but we can't create life. We can chop down an oak tree in twenty minutes, but even with genetic engineering it will take years to grow another one. Generally, destruction is easier than construction. Evil is easier to do than good. Misery is more memorable than happiness. Sorrow is more keenly felt than joy.

I can still remember every shot of the final of the British schools' rackets championship which my partner, Howard Angus, and I – playing for Winchester – lost at Queen's Club in April 1963. I can still recall the moment in the summer of the year before that the wicketkeeper missed a catch off my bowling in a 1st XI game against Charterhouse which, if he'd caught it, might have given us the match. Somehow, and in contrast, one's achievements and victories are filed away in a less noteworthy cabinet called success. Bob de la Motte who now lives in Perth, Australia can give a vivid re-run of the Comrades Marathon in which Bruce Fordyce overhauled him towards the end to win the race. The public only remember the winner – the runner-up remembers the experience.

This asymmetry applies with equal force to gambling. We are all risk-averse, though perversely we like the excitement of gambling, as the popularity of the gaming industry attests. But let's play some mind games to understand the asymmetry in ourselves. If you participate in a lottery or a scratch card game, you know that the odds are minuscule that you will win the R1 million prize. If you're inclined towards mathematics, you will also know that if your ticket costs you R1 there is less than a one-in-a-million chance that you will win such a prize. That's how lotteries and scratch cards make money for charity. The game is biased against you. But you don't mind because it's all in a good cause and you're not going to miss R1 anyway. The reasoning in a casino, where the same condition of unfavourable bias exists, is somewhat different. As a gambler, you feel that provided you don't bet too many times you can beat the statistical laws of probability by good play and luck. It's only if you make a habit of going to the casino every night that you'll lose out in the long run.

However, suppose that a completely new TV game is devised which is a mixture of "The Money or the Box" and SABC's "Win 'n Spin". You have a revolving wheel which has 100 pockets on the perimeter. Fifty pockets are designated "win" and 50 "zero". They alternate with one another. If, when the wheel stops, the ball drops into a "win" pocket you take whatever prize is being offered. If the ball drops into a "zero", you get nothing. The new dimension to the game is this. The compère of the show first announces the size of the prize which can be won on the wheel. He then offers the contestant as an alternative to spinning the wheel a sure sum of cash. The latter he increases until he, the compère, decides to stop. The audience, meanwhile, are giving their advice in no uncertain terms! If the contestant accepts the sure sum at any stage, he forgoes spinning the wheel. If he hasn't accepted the sure sum at the point when the compère stops, he has to spin the wheel.

Let's start with a prize of R10 if the ball drops into a "win" pocket on the wheel. A mathematician will tell you that it makes sense for the contestant to take the option of spinning the wheel unless he is offered a sure sum of R5 or more by the compère. This is because the wheel has a 50/50 chance of success for the contestant, in this case the prize of R10. In mathematical terms, a probability of 50 per cent combined with a R10 prize yields an "expected monetary value" of R5. Another way of arriving at the same conclusion is: if the wheel were spun a million times, chances are that around R5 million would be paid out (R10 on 500 000 occasions and zero on 500 000). That's R5 per spin on average.

Now, let us assume that the sponsor of the show is exceedingly generous because of all the free publicity associated with the show. Instead of the compère offering a R10 prize on the wheel, he offers a R1 million prize. Obviously if R100 is the ceiling of the sure sum on offer, the contestant will spin the wheel.

Equally obviously, if the sure sum rises to R800 000, the contestant will take the sure sum. So where between those two figures will the decision switch? Mathematically, the sure sum on offer at the point of indifference (where the contestant wavers for a long time) is called the "certain equivalent". The "certain equivalent" will vary from person to person – whether he or she is a bit of a gambler or not, married with commitments or single without commitments, well-off or poor and so on. For many ordinary people, nevertheless, the switch from spinning the wheel to the sure sum will occur at well below the mathematician's advice of R500 000.

Think about it yourself. In my case, I'd probably cave in to the sure sum if the compère went to R300 000. The thought of passing up a certain gift of that sum of money if I picked up a "zero" on the wheel would be too painful to contemplate. Interestingly, were one to alter the game to one where several contestants had to bid against each other for the opportunity of spinning the wheel, and the highest bidder actually spun the wheel on the basis that if the ball dropped into a "win" pocket he would be paid the difference between the prize and his bid, and if it dropped into a "zero" pocket he would have to cough up his bid in cash to the sponsor, the amount tendered would be much lower. There is all the difference in the world between a lost opportunity of being given R300 000 and actually parting with R300 000. The idea of losing one's bank balance plus possibly the house, the car and one's other valuable possessions – a wipe-out scenario – would deter most people from wagering a significant proportion of their resources for the privilege of spinning the wheel. Even a substitute wheel having 90 pockets as "win" and ten as "zero" or 95 as "win" and five as "zero" would not lure major sums out of most people. There is an upper limit to what they would be prepared to lay on the line, whatever the prize and whatever the odds (unless the latter were a whisker away from 100 per cent). This example clearly shows that a straightforward mathematical model of how individuals should behave in weighing up the comparative value of uncertain and certain rewards is grossly deficient. The reason is precisely that it ignores the asymmetry of happiness and misery in human psychology.

As far back as 1738, an Italian mathematician named Daniel Bernoulli mooted a game in which a coin was tossed and the prize was awarded in such a way that the "expected monetary value" of the game was infinite, i.e. if someone played the game over and over again, he would become astronomically wealthy. Yet, he knew that a rational person of normal means would only pay a couple of ducats (the Italian currency at the time) to play the game. This contradiction he called the "St Petersburg" paradox. He surmised that people bet on "expected utility value" instead of purely monetary outcomes. "Utility value" is the use to which money can be put in pursuit of happiness. He believed that this was subject to the law of diminishing returns. The first ten ducats brings the winner substantial happiness, the second ten ducats a lesser amount and by the time the winner is a ducat millionaire, an additional ten ducats means virtually nothing. Each extra ducat has progressively less utility attached to it as initially it is spent on necessities whereas latterly it goes towards luxuries. Mathematically, he deduced that the utility value is a logarithmic function of monetary value. If "y" is utility value and "x" is monetary value, they are related to each other in a function where the first derivative dy/dx is always positive, while the second derivative dy^2/dx^2 is always negative. For example, if the prize is increased one-hundred fold from ten ducats to 1 000 ducats (10^3), the utility value of the prize will only rise three times from one to three (replace ducats with cars and you'll see the sense in this reasoning).

Modern utility theory is encapsulated in a book entitled *The Theory of Games and Economic Behaviour*, written in 1944 by Von Neumann and Morgenstern. To the diminishing value of gains on the upside was added the increasing value of losses on the downside. In the "St Petersburg" example, the loss of the first ten ducats would cause some misery, the second ten a whole lot more and depending on the means of the loser further losses would invoke a sense of catastrophe sooner or later. Thus, for an ordinary mortal, the positive utility value of a win of say 100 ducats would fall far short of the negative utility value of a loss of 100 ducats.

A marvellous illustration of this principle of asymmetry occurred in a pub near Putney just before the start of the 1964 boat race between Oxford and Cambridge. Three Cambridge supporters got up on a table and announced to the assembled throng that they would accept any bets – any bets at all – that Oxford would win, since there was no chance of this happening. A colleague of mine from New College, Oxford went up to them and said: "Any bets at all? Fine! £10 000 each." One could see their faces perceptibly change as the thought crossed their minds of what a personal loss of £10 000 would mean, however minuscule the chance. Silently, they climbed down from the table, swallowing their pride (and a few more pints of beer thereafter). The contract was never struck because it would have meant ruin for the loser including my colleague – but he'd made his point! A more familiar example is where a low-mileage, safe driver still insures his car comprehensively, even though he knows that the premium he pays in relation to the sum insured does not reflect the chances of his having an accident, i.e. in purely monetary terms he is paying more than the odds would justify. Obviously, the possibility of taking a heavy financial loss through crashing an uninsured car means more to him than the certainty of parting with a much smaller annual premium. He wants peace of mind.

However, the story that caps all these examples took place in 1986 on the trading floor of one of Wall Street's most famous investment banks. The chairman walked up to the desk of one of the bond traders to play his favourite game of liar's poker. This involves betting on the serial numbers of a dollar bill which each player holds to his chest. Normally, the game was played for a few hundred dollars, but this time the chairman said to the trader: "One hand, one million dollars, no tears." "No," was the response. "If we're going to play for those kind of numbers, I'd rather play for real money. Ten million dollars. No tears." Not even the chairman was up to contemplating a loss of ten million dollars, so he walked away muttering:

"You're crazy." The trader had gambled on this outcome when raising the ante!

In the game of backgammon, as the game progresses one or other player has the option of doubling the bet on the game (with the aid of a doubling cube). If he elects to do so, the other player must either accept the double or accept defeat. If he accepts the former, then he has the right to double the stake at a future point in the game, which puts the pressure back on the first opponent. The cycle can be repeated. Each time the doubling cube is turned, the psychological stress level of the two players must jump exponentially if neither acknowledges defeat. The potential joy over winning twice as much in the event of victory is overshadowed by the potential misery in the event of twice the loss. The widening gap between the two extremes of emotion requires extremely strong nerves. Golfers will sympathise with this situation, knowing the difference between making a short putt for no money and making it for a substantial sum. Suddenly, the distance lengthens, the hole looks smaller and a twitch develops in your wrist!

Another modern development in utility theory is that it has been generalised to explain any type of behaviour which involves a bet, monetary or otherwise. Political leaders tend to fudge issues these days, because clear-cut decisions one way or the other are bound to enrage some or other interest group. This causes so much grief that a compromise with equal misery for all is favoured. In another sphere altogether, a publisher anywhere in the world now has to worry about being politically correct. It has been suggested that George Orwell's book *Nineteen Eighty-Four* only had one thing wrong with it: the title should be have been *Nineteen Ninety-Four*. The point is that increasing sensitivity to political correctness makes publishers more risk-averse. This in turn has led to the shelves of bookshops becoming less and less contentious. Utility theory can explain the boring conformity that is creeping into literature.

On a slightly different note, while manufacturing business these days is run in a more decentralised fashion, the global media industry is becoming more centralised. It is answerable to a handful of magnates focused on the bottom line. Hence, American TV networks no longer air raw coverage from reporters. News has to be filtered through a central ring of producers who, with their eyes on the ratings, re-arrange the facts into an appealing docu-drama. Communiqués are edited into bleached twenty-second sound bytes, the emphasis being shaped by the perceptions and attitude of the ring who are quite happy to act as an internal version of Orwell's Big Brother. The phenomenal rise in the popularity of local talk radio stations which broadcast "live" news and the unabridged, uncensored views of the listeners can be attributed to the risk-averse, politically correct way TV news is now packaged for the public.

In medicine, doctors are increasingly basing their advice to patients on utility theory – knowingly or unknowingly. If you have an operation, they will tell you that these are the odds of success or failure. If you don't have the operation, these are the odds of leading a reasonable life for the foreseeable future. You choose. Indeed, with medical aid schemes decreasing cover to stay viable and health care costs soaring out of control, the sick and infirm are beginning to be faced with the very tough decision of how much they are prepared to pay to keep themselves alive. As one old man put it, the medical profession will eventually make inheritance an obsolete concept.

Another instance where a misery curve is literally in play has been the 1994 World Cup soccer tournament in the United States. The referees showed yellow and red cards to players fouling other players far more frequently than in previous tournaments (the red card leads to instant dismissal from the field, while the yellow card has to be shown twice). The result has been far cleaner games because every player is acutely aware of the potential downside of committing a foul. Who said that raising the odds of punishment and making the punishment more severe does not diminish crime? It certainly works on the soccer pitch!

Each individual has his own utility curve ranking his preferences, distastes and points of indifference. This curve can be made explicit through observation of his betting behaviour or through asking him to make hypothetical judgements on a variety of situations involving pleasure and pain (like the TV auction mentioned earlier). The resulting index can be used to provide an overall perspective of an individual's propensity for risk and the way he is going to gamble in future. An analogy would be the use made by an interior decorator of a spe trum of colour cards to discover exactly his client's favourite colour and shade. A detailed comparison of colours is needed to arrive at the one most preferred.

To demonstrate how individualistic our psychological make-up is regarding risk and reward, consider a mountaineer deciding on whether to ascend to the peak of a mountain the hard way or by an easier route. He is weighing up the extra kudos associated with the more daring climb against the higher risk of injury or death. Since the mountaineering profession tends to attract more risk-tolerant people than other professions, you can be certain that the final judgement will be very different to that of, say, a fit but conservative chartered accountant.

Another interesting example of utility theory at work is a variation of Russian roulette where the five empty chambers of the revolver represent any wish you like whilst the sixth chamber (with the bullet) represents death. Is there any scenario in which a rational individual will take the gamble, spin the revolving cylinder and pull the trigger with a one-sixth chance of death? I guess any loving parent would take the risk for the sake of saving his or her child's life. Very few people would accept the risk for any sum of money unless they were totally desperate or destitute. The broader question is: exactly for what are you prepared to risk laying down your life? It used to be for king and country. Now? The Somalian experience has even got Americans questioning the circumstances under which professional soldiers should risk being killed. Should it only be when their own country is being threatened?

In business, utility theory provides an adequate explanation of entrepreneurial behaviour. In the case of a new gold mine, the higher the upfront sum that has to be invested in opening it, the wider must be the gap between the current gold price and the breakeven gold price at which at least the cash costs of operating the mine are covered. It would be a disastrous scenario if the gold price ever fell to this breakeven level and stayed there, because it would imply that the entire initial capital would be lost (equivalent to the ball dropping into the "zero" pocket of the wheel). Hence, the likelihood of that scenario must be considered virtually nil if a decision to proceed with the mine is taken. The judgement of this likelihood will very much depend on where in an international comparison of cash costs the mine under investigation sits. If it is in the lowest quartile of the cost league, one has a fair degree of confidence that the product price will not fall to the project's breakeven level because most of the industry will be in trouble and shortages will occur. With a very small mining venture, where the percentage of the owner's capital being bet is relatively minor, a higher breakeven gold price can be tolerated. When one has a situation of a breakeven price which is too high for the size of the project, it may still be possible to go ahead by spreading the front-end risk and reducing the amount of capital one puts in oneself. This can be accomplished by bringing partners into a consortium, or the public in a share offer, or putting the project into an existing gold mine with a tax base sufficient to absorb the additional capital expenditure. Tax savings can reduce each gross rand gambled to less than 50 cents net. The front-end exposure is then reduced by over one half.

Finally, let me provide some general advice as to how much of your wealth you should be prepared to bet for different risk/reward ratios:

High risk / high reward	No more than a loss you can live with.
High risk / low reward	None.
Low risk / high reward	A sum where you can feel you're sticking your neck out; but be sure your figures are correct because such opportunities are as rare as hen's teeth.
Low risk / low reward	The widows and orphans option. The more cautious you are, the more you'll like investments of this nature.

Anglo in its history has had several low risk/high reward projects, the most notable of which was the development of the Orange Free State goldfield. The values revealed by the boreholes were consistent and high, the price of gold at the time was stable, inflation rate at two per cent per annum. Conditions were so predictable that, in the Transvaal, Western Reefs paid an unchanged dividend of 25 cents a share for 21 years (1950 to 1970). So Anglo, together with the public via share offerings to them, bet more than its market capitalisation at the time on sinking several shafts simultaneously in the Orange Free State and building the town of Welkom. It paid off handsomely. Given Anglo's market capitalisation today, the equivalent amount would be R50 billion or nearly the cost of the Channel tunnel. By any standards, the OFS mines were an impressive bet!

The nuclear game
is the deadliest of all

In the high-stakes atomic age we live in, the principle of mutually assured destruction ("mad") has played a major role. It rests on the psychology of the misery curve outlined in the previous section. The possibility of achieving victory over your enemy with a pre-emptive nuclear strike has to be balanced against the potential damage he can do to you with a retaliatory nuclear response. The downside associated with the latter, however remote, completely outweighs the upside of the former, however probable. Therefore nobody makes the first move. "Mad" is a bizarre formula for preserving the peace, but it works because it is based on the most fundamental of all human motivations – self-preservation. Indeed, it is ultimately the reason why the "cold war" between the United States and the former Soviet Union never became hot.

"Mad" relied on both superpowers at the time protecting

their second strike capability. The Americans did this through keeping a major portion of their warheads in submarines beneath the ocean, the whereabouts of which were very difficult to pinpoint by the enemy, while the Russians constantly shifted the position of their largest land-based intercontinental missiles at night with the use of mobile launchers. Both sides modified their missiles to carry multiple warheads against which any defence system would have to be astronomically costly to form a completely secure shield. Despite substantially lower arsenals arising from the recent spate of nuclear arms reduction agreements, the "mad" principle remains in force. There is still enough fire power around to level the major cities of both countries. Hence, thorough verification techniques are demanded by each side to establish that the other is not cheating in the disarmament process.

However, there are two new dimensions of the nuclear poker game: one of the two major players is less reliable (Russia) and a multiplicity of new players are seeking a place at the table. The latter development is inevitable given two facts – mankind's lust for power which will never be quenched, and the indestructibility of knowledge. Nobody can rewind history and erase Einstein's equation that energy is the product of mass times the square of the velocity of light. Nobody can destroy the fairly simple handbooks that are now readily available on how to construct an atomic device. In this new game of nuclear poker, which now pits inexperienced hustlers against the old guard, the scope for misjudgment as to the strength of each player's hands has grown dramatically, as has the possibility for bluffing and counter-bluffing. A balancing act is well nigh impossible, suggesting that the biggest players will have to take control of the game. Not easy – particularly when the proliferation of nuclear weaponry raises the odds of a player joining the game with a Samson-like mentality of destroying the entire casino for the sheer hell of it.

Probabilities can be problematic

The Chevalier de Méré was a French gambler towards the end of the 17th Century. He made his living out of rolling a single dice and laying even money with any member of the public who crossed his path that he would throw at least one six in four throws. For reasons known only to himself, he changed his game to rolling two dice and laying even money that he would throw at least one double six in 24 throws. To his dismay the fortune he had accumulated playing the first game started to decline as he played the second one.

He went to his friend, the mathematician Pascal, for an answer to his change in fortune. The latter worked out that one is likely to throw a six in 3,8 throws of a single dice, whereas a double six will probably turn up only once in 24,61 throws of two dice. The chevalier had unwittingly turned the odds against himself. Thereafter he gave up gambling in disgust. Pascal discussed the chevalier's misfortune with a fellow mathematician called Fermat and between them they laid the foundation of the modern theory of probability. Not for nothing is it alternatively called the theory of large numbers. Because the chevalier played the same game over and over again with both the single and the double dice, eventually the laws of probability decided his fate (even though the odds were only fractionally against him when he switched to the double dice).

A casino operates on the same principle. In roulette with one zero, the odds for a player betting on red or black are 37 : 36 against him; in the game of "craps" it is 50,71 : 49,29 against the player. On a single visit customers will only play a limited number of games. Consequently, with odds as close as that a fair number will emerge as winners by having a run of luck. However, from the point of view of the casino where the games are repeated day in, day out, statistics will ultimately prevail in its favour. Conversely, a compulsive gambler has to lose from a series of visits. Nobody can defy probability in the long run even if he is superstitious enough to wear a talisman to bring him luck or bet only on a favourite number.

One must draw the distinction between games broadly of luck which I've just described and games broadly of skill where one is pitting one's wits against other players. These latter games include poker, backgammon and bridge. Here, over the long run, relative expertise will tell and one will beat less experienced opponents. Nevertheless, it's worth knowing the probabilities attached to various events in each game. For example, the odds against being dealt a straight flush in poker are 64 973 to 1, four of a kind 4 164 to 1, a full house 693 to 1, three of a kind 46 to 1, two pairs 20 to 1 and one pair 1,4 to 1. In bridge, the probability of being dealt thirteen cards all of the same suit is one in 158 753 389 900. Four such hands from the same pack would be one in 2 235 followed by 24 additional digits (no wonder that hasn't happened in my lifetime!). On the other hand, there's a slightly better chance than one in five of being dealt a hand with a 4,4,4,3, suit distribution.

None of the above presupposes that someone cannot be dealt an all-of-the-same-suit hand in his or her second game of bridge. But for every time this happens, somebody else has to wait longer than the level of odds suggests, which in an ordinary lifetime means never getting such a hand (the best I've had is nine of the same suit). Expert players at poker and bridge will observe all the cards that have been exposed on the table. Using this information to determine what remains undisclosed, they will revise the odds on the possible combination of cards that can still be played.

Outside of the casino in the world of business, the use of mathematical probabilities becomes much more problematic. Projects are not, like packs of cards, amenable to a theoretical calculation of odds. Nor are they like laboratory experiments which can be repeated many times under identical conditions in order to determine empirically the chances of success or failure. Each project has its special features and takes place in different circumstances. The real world involves economic and political risks which mean prediction of people's behaviour. This is hard to do when you have free will which makes a mockery of trying to achieve the type of precision usually reserved for mechanical events subject to physical laws. The number of potential outcomes to any normal project is vast because of imprecise boundary conditions. No wonder then that entrepreneurs are cynical about attaching specific probabilities to any business outcome. If a professional risk analyst says there's a 63 per cent chance of a project being a success, the entrepreneur will ask: why 63 per cent? Why not 62 per cent or 64 per cent? What evidence is there to suggest such a precise measurement of risk? In the end, it is better to avoid quoting figures and to examine a project under a broad range of scenarios that can be classified as more likely, realistic, less likely or highly unlikely. Never try to narrow the cone of uncertainty that opens up into the future beyond a certain level of approximation or you'll jeopardise your credibility in the eyes of the business community. As soon as you come across as an expert seeking some form of superhuman exactness about the future with charts, graphs and endless computer runs (fake accuracy as one businessman called it), you've lost your audience. Analysis will never be a substitute for "gut feel".

One last point on probability theory is that it is often counter-intuitive. A nice case of an unexpected answer is the one to the question: how many people do you need in a room for there to be at least a 50/50 chance of two of them having the same birthday? Take two people. The probability that the second person will have a different birthday is 364/365. Introduce a third person. There are now only 363 days left, so the probability that he will have a different birthday to the other two is 363/365. The combined probability of the three people not having the same birthday is 364/365 times 363/365. The combined probability that 24 people have different birthdays is: 364/365 times 363/365 . . . times 342/365 equals 0,46. Therefore the probability that two out of 24 people have the same birthday is 1 minus 0,46 equals 0,54 or 54 per cent, i.e. slightly better than 50/50. Armed with this knowledge, like the Chevalier de Méré, you can make a living out of taking bets at cocktail parties of 24 or more by offering even odds that two people there have the same birthday.

Clumsy bluffs get called

Liar dice is a game which requires a considerable talent in bluffing your opponent. The definition in Chambers Dictionary of the word "bluff" is: "to deceive or seek to deceive by concealment of weakness or by show of self-confidence (originally in poker to conceal poor cards)". Liar dice can be played by any number of people sitting in a circle. It involves the normal five poker dice, the throw going clockwise. Each person has to improve on the preceding throw of the player next to him, but keeps his throw concealed from everybody else. He has one throw though he is permitted to keep any portion of the previous throw. If the throw is better than his neighbour's, there is no need to bluff, but he may still inflate his call to make it harder for the next person to beat his hand. If the throw is worse, the player has to bluff that it is better. Any other member of the game can at any stage challenge the truth of a call. If the call was a bluff, the player who gave it has to retire. If not, the challenger has to retire. Eventually, one player is left who scoops the pool.

The secret of success in the game is to try always to give a reasonable call and to be neither a consistent bluffer nor a consistent truth-teller. That way, others are less keen to challenge you because there's more uncertainty surrounding the status of your call (the same is true in poker). The same rules apply to negotiation, whether it's buyers and sellers haggling over the price and terms of a contract or whether employers and trade unions are trying to reach settlement in the annual round of wage negotiations. Take a house sale. We all know that the seller is going to open with a price that there's every possibility that he will reduce if a serious buyer comes along. Equally, a buyer's first offer has every chance of being raised if the seller shows any flexibility at all. An elaborate game of bluff and double-bluff to get to the real bottom line of both parties then takes place. One has final offers, final final offers and I've-absolutely-reached-the-end-of-the-line final offers. The house agent meanwhile plays the role of understanding mediator, coaxing each side towards a deal. Again the process halts if either party indulges in a clumsy bluffing exercise.

Obviously, in a game like liar dice you are expected to lie. But in the real world you are not. "My word is my bond" is an extremely important principle in the free market system. You cannot have lawyers drawing up contracts for everything – it is not only tedious but very expensive. The aforementioned phrase is the motto of The London Stock Exchange, but in essence it applies to the myriad of oral contracts made on a daily basis throughout society. Whether it's a dentist's or doctor's appointment, booking a room at a hotel, ordering an item at a shop, accepting a speaking engagement – each of these obligations has to be fulfilled or adequate notice should be given if circumstances beyond your control intervene to stop you. I remember asking my uncle who was head of a merchant bank in London at the time I lived there in the late 1960s, what was the characteristic he looked for most in promoting somebody to a top management position. His reply: trustworthiness.

Casinos and fellow gamblers don't like cheats either. Ace-up-the-sleeve card sharps and other dishonest types are usually exposed in the course of time and then shunned. In business, "Flash Harrys" come in all shapes and sizes, senior and junior, charming and ugly, with big and little bank balances. They'll trick you out of your money with phoney property deals, "pyramid" schemes and other wonderful ways of making money. Actually, there's no magic in making money. For much of the time, business is a pretty pedestrian affair. As one chief executive put it: "One should remember that an army marches on its stomach. Consequently, good cooks are as vital to the success of a campaign as the tactical skills of the army's commander." He was rightly intimating that the performance of a company rests as much on good teamwork and the blood, sweat and tears of the employees as it does on the quality of decision-making at the top. It is very difficult for commerce and industry (and a casino for that matter) to operate if there are too many cheats around. The descent from failing to keep the small commitments in life via lies and broken promises to major fraud and corruption is only too easy to make. Gamblers – like everybody else – should adhere to a strict moral code.

Nevertheless, one story of cheating from the last century has to be told. At a dinner party, the host who was very wealthy was serving an extremely rare red wine from a crystal decanter. Sitting at the table were a number of guests whom he challenged to name the wine. A young student said he would do so only if, in the event of being correct, he could have the hand of the host's beautiful young daughter. The host was so confident of the wine's rarity that he agreed to the proposal. The student slowly raised his glass to his nose, sniffed the bouquet of the wine, swirled it around in the glass, sniffed it again and sipped it, savouring the taste. With dramatic effect, he intoned the region, then the estate, then the grape and finally the year. He was right on all counts. What the host did not know was that the student and his young daughter were conducting a secret affair. Knowing how proud he was of his wines and his habit of asking his guests to identify them, they had decided that the only way to obtain the father's blessing to their marriage was to set the whole thing up. The daughter had memorised all the details of the wine in the kitchen and passed them on to her lover.

Gamblers are best at betting their own money

Imagine that a friend gives you R1 000 in casino chips as a surprise birthday present. When you go to the tables to play, you will not feel the same about those chips as if you'd purchased them yourself. Since they're a gift out of the blue, the discipline imposed by the negative part of the utility curve associated with losses will be absent. You may well therefore make some rash bets. Gamblers think most efficiently about risk and reward when it is their own money at stake.

Easy money corrodes incentives (if you can get something for nothing, why do anything at all?) and warps the judgement of people who have access to it. Success at school can do exactly the same to the minds of young school-leavers. Forever after, they think that the world will fall into their laps. That's why there's no correlation between performance at school and performance in adult society thereafter.

Take international aid. Apart from much of it being tied to purchases of goods and services from the donor's market, it can ruin the attitude and the market of the country accepting it. In respect of attitude, a country can very quickly turn into an "aid junkie", developing an unshakeable dependency on aid which can only be relieved by regular shots of free cash. In terms of the market, one instantly creates an unfair game in the casino with some people betting their own money and others nothing at all. For example, free food from foreign donors can upset agriculture because it undercuts the price of local farmers' produce (which is their return on the risks they've taken). Dumping of any goods by one country into another has the same unfortunate effects.

Loans (and especially soft loans) are nearly as bad as aid in encouraging the wrong attitudes. Some nations now even borrow money on the basis that they will never pay it back because the maturity dates can be endlessly rescheduled; or they will only do so when the principal value of the loans has been heavily discounted. Such cynicism rebounds on itself because cheats seldom get a second chance to cheat. The sole condition on which overseas aid and loans should be sought and given is where the money can be utilised in good works, passing through as few intermediaries as possible. As a one-off way of financing socially desirable projects and as an alternative to tax rates being boosted to unreasonably high levels, a case can be made for foreign largesse. It may create a false boom in the recipient's economy, but as long as it is recognised as such and the false boom is used as a stepping stone for stimulating self-sustaining economic growth it won't be harmful. If, however, it is utilised for ongoing state expenditure, it removes the discipline required for good government. The sign of a successful country is that most of the cash flowing into it is risk capital in the form of equity finance rather than aid or loans. Then the country knows that it is being looked upon as a casino worth gambling in – one that has honest management and offers reasonable odds.

The principle of instilling proper accountability in people by making them bet their own money is relevant in another context – remuneration structures in business. One of the current management buzzwords is "stakeholders", where one envisages a company adding value to all the raw materials and services it purchases. Some of that added value is retained in the business for new investment opportunities, while the rest is distributed to its own employees as wages, to the state as tax, to lenders as interest and to the shareholders as dividends. All of the latter are therefore stakeholders in the business. The irony of the "stakeholder" approach is that it has come into vogue at exactly the time when many of the stakeholders have forgotten that every business is a gamble. Large companies are viewed as impregnable. Consequently, governments feel free to increase taxes paid by the corporate sector, unions push for wage increases which can be ill afforded and employees react with shock and dismay if the workforce is cut owing to economic conditions. Above all, the costs of employment ratchet up in an inflexible manner with no cognisance being taken of the state of the market.

The only way to reverse this trend is to make all stakeholders more aware of the dynamic nature of world markets with their inherent risks and uncertainties. It's like reminding passengers in large luxury liners, who are unaware of the state of the ocean because of modern stabiliser systems, that the sea can be cruel. This means constant communication between the stakeholders on the commercial realities facing the industry concerned. Specifically, it entails a message that, as in any casino, there are winners and losers and to be a consistent winner requires diligence and application (and sticking to games of chance which have an element of skill). Ultimately, the most effective method of getting this message across to one of the key constituents of the "stakeholder pie" – namely all employees – is to link pay to performance. Production bonuses, profit-sharing schemes, employee share ownership programmes are all conducive to the objective of giving people a material interest in the bottom line.

Another reason why the consciousness of the "casino model" of business is not widespread on the shop floor are the innumerable layers of middle management which cause the workers to be divorced from the raw atmosphere of the gaming tables. That's why so many organisations in the world are stripping out the middle layers; flattening their hierarchies; and turning the shop floor into work teams with greater discretionary powers, and where each individual member is expected to be multi-skilled in order to take on an array of tasks which the team will allocate to him as circumstances dictate.

Gamblers tend to gamble alone. They don't bring along a string of consultants, senior advisers and probability experts. The lesson to be learnt by business is that much wisdom is to be had from the employees themselves once they've been exposed to the market forces. There's no need for intervention by loads of specialist staff who only have a passing acquaintance with the production line and who frequently offer careless advice because it's not their money at stake. Just think how distraught some of them would become if they were paid bonuses and fined according to the accuracy of their forecasts! The shorter the link between the people cutting the commercial deals at the top and the people who have a thorough knowledge of the "boiler room" further down, the better it is for both parties. There has to be a "line of sight" between employees and the market so that they can fully understand what makes business tick.

Betting on credit is risky

Any sane gambler knows that betting on credit is riskier than betting with one's own money. This is particularly so if the credit is being extended by the casino itself and if it is not repaid on time, the debt collectors – weighing in at 120 kilograms a piece – arrive on your doorstep. In Japan, they have an even more effective weapon. Knowing how awful it is to lose face, they send a van with a loud-hailer down your street on a Sunday morning and announce to all your neighbours that not only do you gamble but you are very bad at settling your debts.

Nevertheless, like the governments that become addicted to soft loans described in the previous section, the compulsive gambler always hopes for a better day. The more he sinks into a mire of debt, the more determined he becomes to redeem himself. The misery side of the utility curve which normally limits the downside is suspended. He doubles up. He throws more good money belonging to other people after the bad he has already squandered – till finally fate catches up with him and he disappears, leaving a trail of bad debts behind him. Gamblers always tell you about their wins, but never their losses.

Such an unfortunate fate in gambling is repeated time and again in business. The words sound grander but the story line is the same! Credit is replaced by "gearing", additional credit by "financial restructuring" and the end of the game by "below-the-line write-offs". Distraught bankers send in investigative teams which uncover a can of worms which is invariably far worse than initial indications imply. The smiling tycoon who bewitched them with his charm becomes the villain who swindled them with his exaggerations and lies. A discreet silence settles over the affair as the victims lick their wounds.

Gamblers and businessmen share a common frailty. Sometimes success goes to their heads and they feel they can do no wrong. In Hollywood movies, the star rolls the crap dice and it's seven. He kisses the dice, shakes them in his cupped hands and rolls them a second time; and lo and behold it's seven again. As the crowd gathers around him he repeats this feat over and over. News of the miraculous sequence travels to the casino owner, who appears in a white tuxedo with a worried frown. The lucky hero eventually tires of throwing endless sevens, scoops up a skyscraper-high pile of chips and cashes them in to applause from the audience. The "crash" scenario is never played where, after a few lucky tosses, the star loses the whole lot·instead of quitting while he's ahead.

It is so easy for business moguls to go down the same path. As they become successful (particularly in America), everybody including their own staff starts treating them like deity, never calling into doubt their judgement and never feeding them bad news. They begin believing in their own press. Their ego lifts off like a NASA shuttle and their gambling instinct goes sour. Meanwhile, the financial world is still at their feet, providing them with dollops of capital with only a perfunctory vetting of the projects being funded.

Gearing a project is such an attractive thing to do. In a feasibility study, the raising of loans to offset the initial capital expenditure normally has a wondrous effect on the DCF yield. If the rate of interest on the loan is below the expected DCF yield of the project on an ungeared basis, one can technically drive the DCF yield up to infinity by assuming that sufficient loans will be forthcoming to cover the entire cost of the initial outlays required. "How can this be?" you may ask. Well, something divided by nothing is infinity and in the case of a project fully funded by outside sources, you're not putting up any money yourself. Provided, therefore, some profit net of interest payments on the loan is being projected, you're making a return on a zero input – an infinite return!

The catch in this logic is a point I made earlier in the book. Projected profits have uncertainty attached to them, whereas payments of loan interest and repayment of principal are absolutely certain. It may only require a minor change of the assumptions on which the feasibility study is based for the profit to be wiped out by the interest and the project to go into the red. Yet oh so frequently companies will gear projects up to levels which are quite foolhardy, bearing in mind the risks of the venture. So what is a more prudent approach? The answer lies in equity capital, not loans or debentures. If the party initiating the project does not possess the money itself to pay for it, then rather than trying to retain total control by borrowing the money, a considerably better strategy is to write a prospectus and float the project on the stock market. Thereby the risks are shared among many risk-takers. In the long run, this approach has much less chance of coming to grief. Banks won't break your legs if you don't repay them (or like the Mafia send you to the bottom of the river in cement sandals), but they do have long memories. Reputations lost are never regained.

Charts are an art

Many gamblers go into a casino armed with a notepad and a "system" which will beat the odds. One of the favourites is waiting for a long run of "reds" to occur in roulette because this must increase the odds that the next spin will be "black". But this is a fallacy. The past has no influence on the future. There is no change in the odds on "black" even if 100 successive "reds" were to precede your decision to bet on "black". Indeed, one might begin to think that the "red" notches on the wheel were larger than the "black" notches. In other words, a physical defect had caused the lopsided pattern. With that in mind, it would be more logical to back "red" rather than "black".

Another well-known "system" for beating the bank in roulette is the Martingale. It sounds convincing. You put your money consistently on one colour and double your stakes each time you lose, reverting after a win to your original stake. Thus every time that colour comes up, you will show a net profit of the original stake. The Martingale is indeed close to being a perfect "system", provided your resources are unlimited and the casino will permit a bet of any magnitude. The chances, for example, before you lay down the first stake on "red" of a run of a dozen "blacks" against you are one in 5 096.

Charts appeal in the same way to people playing the stock market or the "derivatives" market. It is felt that they assist in ensuring a successful outcome. Many analysts, however, prefer to look at the "fundamentals" of each share, i.e. the intrinsic worth of that share based on the company's prospects compared to its current share price. They dismiss charts as "voodoo logic". Using them, they say disdainfully, is equivalent to astrologers giving one advice of the type that starts "when Jupiter aligns with Mars". Actually the best indicator of the future behaviour of the Hong Kong stock exchange index has been whether according to the Chinese calendar you're in the year of the dragon or not!

To these allegations, chartists will respond that if sufficient buyers and sellers are following the charts and are triggered into decisions by the way a chart looks, then *ipso facto* they will influence the markets. The favourite term is "resistance level". This is a price point at which much buying and selling has taken place in the past; or it is the ceiling/floor of a trading range established by drawing lines joining previous maxima and minima of the share price. Whichever definition applies, if as the price approaches a "resistance level" its momentum slows down, a reversal of trend is likely. If the price breaches a "resistance level" without slowing down in the process then there is every indication that the trend will not change in the short term but will accelerate.

That's the theory – and indeed if a sufficient number of people are watching a share's behaviour in and around a "resistance level" it would be foolish not to take note too. Should the share price, for example, sink just below the critical figure, a wave of selling orders can be expected. Nevertheless, one has to be careful not to become too mechanistic in one's approach to charts. The classic question is: when is a trend not a trend? The answer is: when it's a turning point. This implies that you can only find out in retrospect whether a reversal has taken place. All traders have brilliant 20/20 hindsight! Often a share rises or falls over a long period of time with minor fluctuations along the way. It is these minor fluctuations that catch you out.

Of relevance here is the recent advance in the field of mathematics called "chaos theory" or "fractals". Mathematicians have shown that economics and markets, as well as the weather, have non-linear properties. This means that they are all complex mixtures of stable and unstable factors and it is impossible to determine in advance which will predominate. Indeed, for infinitesimally small changes in the starting conditions, the system can tend towards equilibrium, or spontaneously transform itself into something completely new. In other words, the only sound advice one can give in non-linear circumstances is to be adaptable and creative as events unfold.

I think, though, that my fundamental caution about charts stems from the fact that completely contradictory signals can be given by them, depending on one's interpretation of them. Two models used to interpret charts come to mind: the "momentum" and the "overbought/oversold". The former one says that if a share price is trending strongly in one direction, it will intersect certain important lines like the moving daily average, monthly average and so on. Once it does that, it implies that the positive/negative momentum the share has will be difficult to stop. The share under this model becomes a firm "buy" if it is rising and "sell" if it is falling – in other words "go with the flow". The "overbought/oversold" model on the other hand asks one to imagine that the share price is attached to its average over any length of time by a rubber band. The more the price moves away from the average, the stronger will be the return pull. Hence, once it has broken a few moving average lines, it is moving into a dangerously overbought or oversold situation. This gives precisely the opposite signal of the other model in terms of action to be taken: "buy" on a fall, "sell" on a rise – in other words "be a contrarian".

The art lies in choosing which model is relevant at different moments in a share's history. Years of accumulated experience give you that intuitive instinct. Companies have long learning curves in finding the best and cheapest way to produce a product. Likewise, fund managers need a few bull/bear cycles to hone their judgement on which way the market is going. You won't always be right as an experienced gambler, but you'll be right more often than not.

Advice to gamblers comes in threes

If you have read this book carefully, you will have come across two sets of golden rules about facing uncertainty in business and in life generally – both in triplets.

The first triplet is fairly obvious:
– assess the risk;
– review the potential reward; and
– in view of the estimated risk and reward decide the proportion of your assets you wish to gamble.

Hollywood, for example, now produces endless sequels to movies which, in their original form, were massive hits. The reasons are contained in this first triplet. The risk of a sequel is less than that of a fresh film. The reward of a sequel can be as large as – if not larger than – that associated with the original hit. Finally, because of the enormous increase in a film's production costs, a greater proportion of a film company's assets is being invested in each individual production than, say, 20 or 30 years ago. Hence, on weighing up the risk versus the reward, a film company tends to favour sequels wherever possible because they're a safer bet.

The second triplet is more interesting but was somewhat concealed within the text:

- play multiple scenarios and in particular keep opposites in mind;
- look for peripheral opportunities and threats that may become central to your existence over the next five or ten years; and
- work out carefully what you can and you cannot control to exact maximum leverage out of what you can control and adapt to what you can't.

Let me end with three analogies which reveal the common sense contained in the latter triplet. The first analogy concerns agriculture. A farmer knows the weather is uncertain and he therefore has to play multiple scenarios for each season – early rains, late rains, too much rain, drought. As the season progresses he will instinctively change the probabilities on each of these scenarios and act accordingly. Secondly, he will also know, if he is a far-sighted farmer, what peripheral opportunities and threats face his farm. Perhaps they'll be in the form of scientific developments in fields like biotechnology. Alternatively, they may arise from long-term shifts in taste which affect the livestock, cereal or vegetable trade. Or it could be the implications of long-term environmental trends such as desertification, drying-up of water sources and global warming. Thirdly, he understands perfectly what he does and he doesn't control. The seeding time, the rotation of crops and fields, the selection of fertilisers, the type of agricultural equipment, the quality control of his product, the motivation of his workforce – these are things over which he has mastery. The weather he cannot change.

The second analogy is a legal one and focuses on the point about keeping opposites in mind. In the courtroom at the beginning of a trial, two scenarios are going through the head of the judge about the defendant – that he is innocent or guilty. Evidence is led by the prosecution and defence which, as the trial proceeds, sways the judge towards one or the other scenario. At the end, he plays the "innocent" and "guilty" scenarios against one another – weighing up all the evidence – and delivers the verdict. Now, in the case I am citing here, the "multiple scenario" thinking of the judge is considered obligatory for the role he is performing. If he were to adopt a more single-minded approach, he would be considered an unsuitable judge. Yet, this entire example concerns the interpretation of the past. We know even less about the future than the past. Hence, it makes even greater sense to adopt a flexible approach towards the future along the lines advocated in this book. The case rests!

The third analogy is a yachting one. Consider a lone yachtsman who is sailing his yacht across the Atlantic from Halifax in Nova Scotia to Southampton in England. Depending on daily weather conditions, he will zig and zag and even at times retrace his route, but in the longer run he will pursue a course which gets him closer to his destination – Southampton. In other words, his operational flexibility in no way contradicts his overall objective. Of course, he may abandon the trip altogether if weather conditions become too extreme, but even that makes sense since he doesn't want to sink his yacht at all costs.

In terms of the first rule of "multiple scenarios" and "keeping opposites in mind", like the farmer, the yachtsman is not an expert in predicting what the weather is going to be like tomorrow. But he is an expert in knowing the correct response to all possible weather patterns and in gauging the opportunities and threats that arise from each situation. His experience lies in assessing the probabilities of different weather patterns that may evolve over the next 24 hours, deciding on an optimal sailing strategy within that range of short-term probabilities and implementing it swiftly and effectively. He is constantly playing multiple scenarios, placing different odds on each scenario as the trip progresses, making decisions while keeping options open, gambling on his instinct, measuring the risk versus the reward of each move, reversing moves where failure is becoming apparent. The process is very dynamic but in no way indecisive.

As regards the second rule of scanning the horizon, no doubt any good yachtsman these days is assisted by radar and is supported by a team, based on land, tracking global and regional weather patterns. If there is a gale warning, he'll know about it well in advance of the gale's arrival and will take appropriate action either to avoid it or to batten down the hatches. Lighthouses still act as an important peripheral sign of land approaching. Sudden "wild card" scenarios such as the tearing of a sail, the snapping of a mast or the capsizing of the boat have all been played through the yachtsman's mind. Contingency plans are in place to minimise the negative impact of such eventualities. In a trans-oceanic race, the art of re-perception comes into play, since the likely winner is the contestant who can exploit in the most original manner the combination of current and swell together with wind magnitude and direction.

The third rule of distinguishing between what you can and cannot control is underlined by one obvious fact that every yachtsman knows: he cannot control the weather or the conditions of the sea. He can only react to the environment. It is quite amusing to note that if a corporate team with a "single desired future" mentality were crewing the yacht, the first assumption they would make in any planning session would be a following wind and a tranquil sea. Moreover, the yacht would have to be modified to cope with the overhead of a strategic operations room, making it heavier, less responsive, slower and probably less seaworthy!

Basically, the yachtsman controls the yacht, but even there the design and technology of the yacht places limitations on what he can do with it. Nevertheless, the principle of "leverage" I was describing earlier is superbly demonstrated by *Australia II*'s remarkable win in the America's Cup in 1983. By means of fairly small modifications to the keel, the designer of *Australia II* produced a significant improvement in performance which, given how close the contest was between the Australians and the Americans, was the difference between victory and defeat.

The yachtsman epitomises the message I have been trying to convey throughout this book on gambling. When one man is pitting his skill against the elements, when his bouts of boredom because conditions are calm are interspersed with terrifying changes in those conditions which require the best in him to survive, when small modifications in his tactics or his craft can literally mean the difference between life and death, when flexibility in daily strategy in no way conflicts with the fixed objective of arriving at the final destination, you have a model of thinking which is extremely effective in the art of daily living. Uncertainty should not be denied. It should be positively embraced. That is the attitude which will empower individuals to turn dreams into possibilities and turn the best of possibilities into realities. By closing your mind and focusing totally on a "single desired future", you might make it through the rapids, but don't count on it. The natural faculties you possess to keep opposites in mind, maintain peripheral vision and distinguish between what you can and cannot control are the most precious assets any human being can have to cope with change. Don't let anybody persuade you to drop these natural abilities in favour of a more dogmatic approach. Original ideas usually start out by being half-baked before they become fully baked enough to challenge orthodox beliefs.

Life is a constant adventure. The freedom to choose between alternative futures as this adventure unfolds is about the most important freedom you have. Guard it, nurture it and above all use it to shape your life in the best manner imaginable while you wend your way through this uncertain world.